SYMBOLIC SIT-INS

Protest Occupations at the California Capitol

John Lofland
Michael Fink

UNIVERSITY
PRESS OF
AMERICA

To Jackie Habecker,
Champion of Civility,
who dealt with it all.

CONTENTS

PREFACE

We seek here to analyze an emerging form of social movement protest action, one we observed for several years at the California State Capitol, and one which may acquire considerable significance in the social struggles of the eighties.

We label it the "symbolic sit-in" referring, roughly, to protest occupations or "seizures" of places or spaces that draw on the ideology, rhetoric and posture of historic sit-ins but which lack the classic, additional earmarks of those actions; namely, true disruption of the settings in which they occur, an atmosphere of crises, the threat of (and actual) violence, and extensive involvement by bystanders and other third parties.

The symbolic sit-in is but one new and special form of protest and in our opening chapter we strive to set it in larger and comparative perspective. This is followed by an explanation of the symbolic sit-in itself, a depiction of the setting in which we observed many episodes of it, and an overview of the five major variations it, in turn, displays. The core chapters provide detailed descriptions of each of these five "types," the pack-in, lone-in, one night stand, spirited siege, and long term vigil. We conclude with observations on the dynamics of the symbolic sit-in, its possible effectiveness, future, and related matters.

We hope this report might be of use to several audiences, an ambition that often ends in satisfying no audience but an outcome we endeavor to avoid in this instance. As the theorizing in Chapter I makes clear, our paramount aim is to advance the general analysis of protest by contributing to the rapidly evolving bodies of materials grouped under the rubric "collective behavior and social movements" by sociologists and the heading "interest group politics" by political scientists. But even though scholars of these topics are our main, intended audience, we think both "protesters" and "authorities"—the abstract antagonists who people these pages—might draw useful insights from the experiences we chronicle and discuss. On the protester side, <u>Symbolic</u> <u>Sit-ins</u> can be read as a manual of action-options and associated contingencies in a number of political contexts. On the authority side, a variety of tactics of control and negotiations for certain kinds of challenges are readily apparent. In view of the fact that protesters and authorities are, by definition, in conflict the seeming neutrality of offering aid to both may appear cynical or manipulative. Such, however, is not the case. We are, in point of fact, personally more sympathetic with protesters than authorities much of the time. We simply recognize that accurate data and valid analysis can be put to advantage by anyone who elects to learn them, irrespective of their social location in a conflict.

By its nature, this research has necessitated the active help, solicitude or at least indulgence of a large number of people, often at times when they were coping with stressful situations. We have a great debt to all those involved and we are pleased to be able here to extend our thanks to them.

The senior author wants in particular to acknowledge the "license to be present" and the active assistance given him by members of the Deaf/Blind and Title XX Coalitions. Additionally, he desires to thank the California State Police for an official "license to be present" at protest events. The cordiality of a number of members of the State Police, especially the Commander of the Governor's security force, is also much appreciated.

The longest, most intense and complicated of events we report—the PUARS vigil described in Chapter VI—necessitated more than ordinary assistance from participants in chronicling it and the junior author offers special thanks to the several members who helped him extensively during the vigil and provided detailed post-vigil interviews.

Michael Greany superbly assisted the senior author over the summer of 1977 and his notes are drawn on in reporting aspects of some episodes. He was the prime observer of the farm worker "pack-in" described in section A of Chapter III.

The 1977 portion of the research was supported in part by two small grants from the Davis Division of the University of California Academic Senate, by a Faculty Associate Appointment with the Institute of Governmental Affairs at Davis, and by sabbatical leave from the Davis Department of Sociology.

Throughout the project, Professor Lyn H. Lofland provided much needed and enormously appreciated boosting and support of morale and incisive observations and suggestions. She, more than anyone else, made the research possible.

Doris Craven typed a draft of the manuscript and Computerized Typing Service, Davis, California, prepared text for the publisher. We are highly appreciative of their skills and precision.

This book is dedicated to Jackie Habecker, with admiration, for the reasons given in section D of the concluding chapter.

John Lofland
Michael Fink

CHAPTER I

SOCIAL STRUGGLE AND THE PROTEST OCCUPATION

In this report we depict and dissect a series of "sit-ins" and associated events centered on the reception room of the Governor's office at the Capitol of California over the six years 1975-1980. In comparing the pattern of these protests with other forms of social struggle, we have come to conceive it as the "symbolic sit-in" or more technically the "symbolic protest occupation" (occupation meaning occupancy, not employment). It is a new form of protest that we believe will be an increasingly used and significant tool in the tactical kits of social movements in the eighties.

In order best to present the nature and import of the symbolic sit-in we begin by sketching the larger picture in which it appears as a somewhat secondary but nonetheless important feature. That is, objects have meaning only as a function of context and we begin by supplying it.

A. THE THREE FUNDAMENTAL FORMS OF SOCIAL STRUGGLE

Complex societies are vast and intricate arenas of social struggle—of politics in that term's most fundamental meaning—over the distribution of the scarce resources of class, status and power. In what are, by definition, "ordinary times" the dominately employed strategy of struggle is "orderly" and "polite." Its earmarks are restraint, staidness, dignity and diplomacy. Its ideals are codified in Robert's <u>Rules of Order</u> and Emily Post's <u>Etiquette</u>.

One of the most important modes of its organization is the <u>interest group</u> and three major patterns of such groups' polite activities have been identified as lobbying, representation in decision-making, and "comprehensive mobilization" in which the group and its members are integrated into a wide variety of contexts (Salisbury, 1975:206-218). In the narrowly political realm, tactics of polite struggle include cultivation of personal ties, assembly and distribution of "analyses" and "data" supportive of one's interests, media campaigns, and monetary support of people who can and do help one's group (as in political contributions) (Ornstein and Elder, 1978:53ff). Phrased more abstractly, the devices of polite struggle are persuasion and bargaining (Turner, 1970). And even though many tactics may be illegal—as in bribery, blackmail, wiretapping and burglary—these are carried on in a physically peaceful, courteous and circumspect manner.

For complicated and concatenated reasons, themselves surrounded by centuries of often acrimonious debate, at least some contenders in the arena of society engage, on occasion, in protest or violent struggle, the two fundamental alternatives to polite struggle.

Violent struggle refers, of course, to the strategy of physically damaging or destroying property or other humans. Its more "primitive" (in the sense of relatively unplanned and short-lived) forms include proletarian and bourbon lynchings, mob attacks, communal and ghetto riots, pogroms and official riots. More sophisticated (in the sense of planned and long-lived) forms include the bombings and kidnappings of terrorists bands, guerrilla armies, insurrections, dual sovereignty contests, and international war.

Protest struggle stands between polite and violent struggle, a kind of "middle force." As we use the term, protest eschews or at least avoids the extensive physical damage to property and humans found in violent struggle on the one side and the restraint decorum of staid politics on the other. It is an "out of place" form of struggle in at least the two senses of often being conspicuously out-of-doors or impolitely and ostentatiously intrusive on indoor space. The garden variety form of protest struggle is the "demonstration," defined by Webster as "the act of making known or evident by visible or tangible means" and a "public display of group feeling." In ordinary usage over recent decades there are connotations of "uninstitutionalized" and "street" actions. Thus, one analyst properly distinguishes demonstrations from "more routine forms of expression, such as regular participation in a town meeting or party convention" (Etzioni, 1970:4).

Our usage includes but is not coextensive with what is called "nonviolence" or "nonviolent action" as those terms were employed in the American civil rights movement of the nineteen sixties (e.g., Bell, 1968) and have been reflected on by philosophers (e.g., Stiehm, 1972).

Protest is a broader and more generic phenomenon and antedates nonviolent protest by millenia. A signal feature is, rather, an impatience with the encumberances of institutions and a readiness to act impolitely but not necessarily with violence.   Howard Zinn and Kenneth Clark capture this quality when describing 'the early ethos of the Student Nonviolent Coordinating Committee (SNCC).   As Zinn and Clark are quoted in Piven and Cloward (1977:222), SNCC participants had

> "...an eagerness to move out of the political maze of normal parliamentary procedure and to confront policy-makers directly with a power beyond orthodox politics—the power of people in the streets and on the picket line" [Zinn, 1964:13] . And Clark said that "SNCC seems restless with long-term negotiation and the methods of persuasion of the Urban League, and it assumes that the legislative and litigation approach of the NAACP" had exhausted its possibilities [Clark, 1966:259] .

These distinctions among polite, protest and violent politics or struggle have considerable precedent in the literature, albeit little elaborated. They seem, for example, much the same as the distinctions Arthur I. Waskow has drawn among the politics of order, violence, and "creative disorder" in analyzing the American civil rights movement of the early sixties.

> In the politics of order, people divide their attention between the changes to be accomplished and the accepted rules of society about the "legitimate" ways of bringing about change. In the politics of violence, people divide their attention between the changes to be accomplished and those powerful people who get in the way of change—the enemy. In the politics of disorder, people tend to reduce greatly their interest in both the given rules and the enemy; instead they focus very strongly on the changes to be accomplished. To oversimplify a bit, in the politics of order, [people] ...follow the rules; in the politics of violence, they attack their enemies; in the politics of disorder, they pursue change [Waskow, 1966:277-278] .

Or, in treating "direct action," (i.e. protest) British political theorist April Carter marks it off "from guerrilla warfare and street fighting...[and from], at the other end of the scale....political activity relying on speeches, leaflets and general propaganda which are the stock in trade of constitutional pressure groups...[The latter] may well be a prelude to direct action, or an ancillary aspect...but they are not in themselves a form of [it], unless undertaken as a challenge to specific laws or the authorities" (Carter, 1973:24).

The important task, of course, is not merely to reiterate these distinctions but to forge on in making analytic use of them.

B. TYPES OF PROTEST STRUGGLE

If we want to understand protest struggle, we need first (or at least early-on) to draw a reasonably clear picture not just of it as a global entity but as a complexly constituted creature composed of numerous forms. To what kinds of actions (as well as situations and definitions of them) are we referring when we evoke the notion of protest? As obvious as this question may be, relatively little systematic attention has been accorded it. Ralph Turner's (1970) briefly drawn contrasts among persuasion, bargaining and coercion seem all too easily to suffice for most analysts (e.g., Zald and McCarthy, 1979). The single most concerted effort has been that of Gene Sharp in his monumental The Politics of Nonviolent Action (1973), a work remarkably disattended by scholars but studied and used quite seriously in some contemporary social movements.

Drawing on and modifying Sharp, we propose four major classes of protest politics, four classes that can themselves be ranked from "lower" to "higher" levels of system-challenge and social definition of seriousness.

At the first and lowest level is symbolic protest, those orderly and nondisruptive but more or less ostentatious ways in which people collectively draw attention to their grievances. Sharp (1973:Ch. 3) treats this class under the label "nonviolent protest and persuasion," calling attention to ways in which such actions also overlap with the devices of polite politics. April Carter (1973:24) also views symbolic protest as "on the borderline of direct action," as is evident in the quote from her, just above. And, in the contemporary anti-nuclear movement one encounters a distinction between "direct and symbolic action," the former often held to be superior to the latter (Chatfield, 1980:7).

The three prime forms of symbolic protest are the procession (e.g., marches, parades), the assembly (e.g., the rally) and various kinds of public acts, including picketing. Sharp (1970:Ch. 3) lists fifty-four detailed forms of it that he groups, in part, into formal statements, group presentations, symbolic public acts, drama, and honoring the dead.

It needs to be stressed that these "modest," or even almost polite protest actions are such only in the context of relatively open societies; that is, they are symbolic because authorities and other citizens are prepared to allow people to perform acts that can be symbolic without hinderance. The "symbolic" nature of the protest resides in the social response to it and not only in the act itself. To the degree that audiences define what could be symbolic protest as threatening and as something that must be stopped or interferred with, to that degree the protest act escalates to a third class we will discuss, the "intervention." One classic illustration is the response of authorities to civil rights paraders in Birmingham, Alabama in early 1963 and Selma, Alabama in early 1965. Mere symbolic protest (parading) achieved the status of intervention protest by virtue of authorities electing to define parading as intervention (Garrow, 1978).

The second basic form of protest is non-cooperation, a refusal to provide the actions necessary for a social arrangement to continue. Sharp declares that nonviolent action "overwhelmingly" involves this class and 103 of the 198 methods he describes in his book are so classified. He in turn divides them into their social, economic or political focus (devoting a chapter to each). The most familiar are in the economic realm, including, of course, the strike, the slowdown and the boycott and variations on them.

Sharp's third and final class of protest action—the intervention—encompasses two forms we feel ought to be distinguished. We will describe what is for us the fourth, final, and highest form of protest (the alternative institution) prior to the third (the intervention) because we will hereafter not be returning to the fourth and it will only clutter discussion to come back to it. Sharp's distinctions between "negative" and "positive" forms of intervention seem to us more fundamental than simply a variation on intervention, the way in which he elects to deemphasize the distinction. He defines "positive intervention" as establishing "new behavior patterns, policies, relationships, or institutions which are preferred" (Sharp, 1973:357). Following his usage, this class can be labeled alternative institutions, subforms of which include alternative communication, transportation, and economic systems and "dual sovereignty and parallel government" (Sharp, 1973:Ch. 8). To the degree that the protest alternative institution comes to supersede the loyalties of citizens, this is the most serious and consequential type of protest. It can augur quite profound—even revolutionary—change in ways not possible in connection with the other three major classes of protest.

The third basic form (for us), the intervention, may "disrupt or even destroy established behavior patterns, policies, relationships, or institutions which are seen as objectionable" (Sharp, 1973:357). As Sharp mentions (1973:357), compared to symbolic protest and non-cooperation, "methods of...intervention pose a more direct and immediate challenge." They seem, indeed, more prone to involve violence.

Somewhat reordering Sharp's treatment, four patterns of intervention may be distinguished:

1)   harassment, in which the objectionable activities of a person (or an objectionable person) are (is) continually called attention to in some out-of-the-ordinary manner;

2)   system overloading, in which a too large amount of whatever an arrangement processes is injected;

3)   blockade, in which protesters temporarily impede the movement of objectionable people and/or materials (e.g., Taylor, 1977); and,

4)   occupation, in which people "enter or refuse to leave some place where they are not wanted or from which they have been prohibited" (Sharp, 1973:371).

C. THE PROTEST OCCUPATION

The fourth class of intervention, the occupation, is most germane to understanding the symbolic sit-ins that are the central subject of this report. Only slight reflection is required to appreciate that, in twentieth century America, the protest occupation has constituted the leading edge technique of at least four major social movements and has been an important ancillary device in several others (as well as being an unsung but integral aspect of all American history; see, for example, Cooney and Michalowski, 1977). In sequence, the four major "waves" of this century have been as follows.

(1)   Among industrial workers in the thirties, "sit down strikes" were the practice of "taking over" plants or other work places as a tactic in winning union recognition and other advances.   Starting sporadically in the early thirties, their number escalated and they became a "fashion" of a sort in 1936 and 1937, jumping from 48 affecting 88,000 workers in 1936 to 477 affecting 400,000 workers in 1937. One newspaper remarked on this "strike storm" that "sitting down has replaced baseball as a national pastime, and sitter-downers clutter up the landscape in every direction" (quoted in Fine, 1979:331). This technique was augmented by the ordinary strike and pickets, of course, but some analysts have argued that success of the "vast labor upheaval" of the thirties was centrally dependent on the use of the sit-down (Piven and Cloward, 1977:Ch. 3; Fine, 1979:338-341).

(2)   Likely most memorable is the use of the "sit-in" by the civil rights movement in 1960-61, a wave of public accommodation broachings that in a year and a half involved "at least 70,000 sit-inners" in "over a hundred cities and towns in every southern and border state..." (Matthews and Prothro, 1966:23). Here, also, some observers have claimed that the sit-in as a technique was a critical component of success, although obviously augmented by boycott and parading (Piven and Cloward, 1977:Ch. 4).   Indeed, the "sit-in" was such an integral part of the civil rights movement that the name of the technique has often been used interchangeably with the substantive name of the movement!

(3) Not quite as sharp in the collective memory is the fact that participants in the student movement of the middle and late sixties quite often seized buildings as part of their strategy. Beyond the famous episodes at Berkeley in 1964 ("where it all began") (Heirich, 1971) and Columbia in 1968, hundreds of campus buildings were occupied over the years of the late sixties. Bayer and Austin (1971:307) report almost three hundred were seized/blockaded in <u>each</u> of the years 1968-69 and 1970-71.

(4) After several years of relative disuse, the basic technique was taken up by the anti-nuclear movement in the late seventies, continuing into the early eighties. While no firm figures are yet available (in part because media have elected to downplay or ignore the movement's existence and protest actions [Gitlin, 1980:287ff]), successful and attempted occupations of nuclear-involved places have numbered at least in the hundreds since 1974 and have involved many thousands of protesters (Barkan, 1979).

We might think of these as four major "waves" of protest occupations within which and between which smaller eddies and swirls have also occurred. There are, thus, the Native American occupations at Alcatraz Island in 1969, at Wounded Knee in 1973, and at a variety of other places (Editorial Research Reports, 1978:13-14). In 1977, groups of disabled occupied several offices of the Federal Government, one of them for 26 days (Anderson, 1977:49). And, there have been a host of other efforts, many of them quite localized and brief (see, e.g., Cooney and Michalowski, 1977).

Thus summoned up, let us consider, first, some important ways these waves vary and, second, key features they have in common that set them off from, but informing of, the symbolic sit-ins to which we will come in the next chapter.

We believe it is important to distinguish among protest occupations in terms of the relation between the territory seized and the protest demands being made. In what we might consider the most primordial of relations, the protesters lay an <u>ownership</u> claim to the exact territory they have elected to seize. Such has been the case for numerous Native American protest occupations. Up slightly from that, the occupation lays a claim to the <u>use</u> of a place or at least to a place of that <u>kind</u> if not that exact place. The Squatters Movement in Britain following World War II, in which the homeless occupied empty houses without legal sanction, illustrates this variation (Carter, 1973:16ff). In both, there is an integral or substantive relation between the act of occupation and the place occupied.

These differ from the pattern in which a place is temporarily occupied in order to press for expanded public rights of <u>access</u>. In the classic sit-ins of the civil rights movement white seats of lunch counters, churches, bus stations and the like were occupied to gain the quite concrete right to occupy the specific seat where situated and all seats of "that sort." Here, too, there was an integral and immediate relation between the protest act and the objective of the protest act. Wade-ins, ride-ins and so forth were genotypically identical in this way although phenotypically quite different.

Next, territory can be brought under protester control for the purpose of promoting a demand that lies beyond and is substantively disconnected from the territory occupied. The sit-down capture of factories in the American thirties was, thus, not an effort to seize the ownership of factories or to gain a right to be in a factory but only a device to strengthen one's bargaining position. Student seizure of buildings in the sixties were likewise efforts to gain leverage in struggles with campus officials rather than efforts to live in administration buildings (an ownership claim) or to gain the right to enter such buildings (a rights claim). Both were tactical in nature.

Last, in what might be thought as a very elaborate variation on the blockade, territory can be occupied for the purpose of preventing an objectionable activity from starting or continuing at that place. As in the initial three patterns above, there is a substantive relation between occupation and territory but it is of a quite different character, at least in the case of anti-nuclear activists who are its main practitioners. No ownership or rights claim is made on a nuclear site, but the site and the protest act are nonetheless substantively connected because the nuclear activists are directly acting against a place to which they object because of its constitutive activity.

As we will spell out below, the symbolic sit-ins we observed at the California Capitol were exclusively of the type we term tactical. No claims of ownership, access rights, or constitutive objections were made.

An appreciation of protest occupation history, waves, and variations in the relation of occupation to demand, help us now to see a number of ways in which these episodes are also similar despite their manifest differences. These need to be elaborated because they provide a set of contrasts with symbolic sit-ins; that is, symbolic sit-ins do not have these features and their absence is central to understanding them.

(1) An initial matter has already been mentioned but its significance has not been drawn out. Protest occupations tend to occur in "waves," or spurts that last only two to a few years. All parties to them tend to bracket individual episodes together as "part" of a class of events "of this kind" that "we are experiencing now." In sheer statistical terms, only a few episodes are perceived as "isolated" or "minor."

(2)   This wave quality is not a matter of mere, dispassionate cognition.   Everyone involved defines the developing wave situation as one of challenge and crisis.   Unusual numbers of police or even the military are likely to be mobilized or at least action to do so agonized about by some and demanded by others.   On all sides, emotions become highly aroused and the rhetoric inflated.

(3)   Standing patterns of setting activity tend in fact to be disrupted: factories stop running; lunch counters stop serving; college administrations stop functioning; construction crews stop building.

(4)   The occupations are defined as "third party relevant" in several senses.   "Everyone" in public life, especially people in political offices, feel they can and should pronounce on the occupations, especially on their legality.   Segments of local populations feel it is appropriate for them to appear at the occupation site and openly to comment on the proceedings, either hostilely or sympathetically.   Mobs may harass the occupiers; supporters may develop elaborate support organizations (as in the extraordinary General Motors sit-down strike of 1936-37); crowds may do battle with police or military deployed to eject the occupiers. Irrespective of the content, there is enormous on and off-the-scene third party action and attention (Fink, 1980).

In composite, features such as these make up what sociologists refer to as a "collective behavior situation," a situation in which people collectively move toward:

1)   Defining a situation as extra-ordinary and as reason for suspending the "attitude of everyday life" and the ordinary sense that "nothing unusual is happening" in favor of a definition that "something unusual is happening;"

2)   displaying high levels of emotional arousal and, in particular, high levels of fear, hostility and joy; and,

3)   acting in ways that are socially defined as unusual, among occupiers, authorities, and others and aside from and in addition to the unusual acts that constitute the protest occupation per se (Lofland, 1981:411-417).

The pattern thus described is the true protest occupation or more loosely, the classic sit-in or territorial seizure.   It has at least two kinds of significance for what follows, for an understanding of the symbolic protest occupation.   One, for reasons to be elaborated, the symbolic sit-in is a variety of symbolic protest—the first or "lowest" class of protest outlined above—and not a type of non-cooperation, intervention or alternative institution—the other three classes.   Two, it became possible for the symbolic sit-in to emerge and to enter the repertoire of social movement protest actions precisely because of the background of waves of protest occupation just described. Those waves (and eddies) provided the imagery and the rhetoric of protest that inspired the crystallization of the symbolic sit-in.

===

We may conclude this context-setting introduction by calling attention to the social importance of what may be thought of as "protest studies." Without arguing the reasons, we may take as a working premise the generalization that polite politics seem unable effectively to respond to the churnings and grindings of modern societies. Violent and protest politics keep appearing, albeit sporadically and in waves. If the world cannot be made safe for and by polite politics and if violent and protest politics seen unavoidable or even inevitable, a key question becomes not if but in what form and in what manner? Once beyond polite politics, the initial choice is obviously between protest and violent politics.

For scholarly analysts such as ourselves who prefer protest to violent politics in most circumstances, a priority concern becomes that of how to facilitate the former and inhibit the latter. One way to foster the choice of protest politics is to provide increasingly articulate, wide-ranging, and usable analyses of it, analyses that are empirical, reflective, and systematic. Oddly, despite endless journalistic reports, moral musings and abstract theorizings, there are few studies displaying these scholarly features, features of empirical closeness and analytic acuity.

Happily, however, a viable field of something like "protest studies" does seem to be on the horizon (e.g., Zald and McCarthy, 1979; Tilly, 1979) and we can envision a day when scholarly treatment of protest achieves the same institutional embodiment and support as already enjoyed by the study of polite and violent politics (and which we dare say encourages each of them). (One not so whimsical possibility is, indeed, university departments and institutes of protest studies, paralleling current departments and institutes of political science that ought more accurately be labeled departments and institutes of polite politics.)

We are suggesting, then, that, paradoxically, the social arena is made more stable and workable by means of protest and that one important task of social analysts is to facilitate at least some forms of it by means of activist-utilizable scholarly analyses. It is to that larger end that this report is directed.

REFERENCES

Anderson, Maurice
    1977   "Power to the Crips!" *Human Behavior*, July, pp. 48-49.

Barkan, Steven
    1979   "Strategic, Tactical and Organizational Dilemmas of the Protest Movement Against Nuclear Power." *Social Problems* 27:19-37.

Bayer, Alan E. and Alexander W. Astin
    1971   "Campus Unrest, 1970-71: Was It Really All that Quiet?" *Educational Record* 52:301-313 (Fall).

Bell, Inge Powell
    1968   *Core and the Strategy of Nonviolence.* New York: Random House.

Carter, April
    1973   *Direct Action and Liberal Democracy.* New York: Harper and Row.

Chatfield, David
    1980   "Direct Action in the UK." *It's About Times*, August, p. 7.

Clark, Kenneth B.
    1966   "The Civil Rights Movement." *Daedalus* 95:250-260 (Winter).

Cooney, Robert and Helen Michalowki (eds.)
    1977   *The Power of the People: Active Nonviolence in the United States.* Culver City, CA.: Peace Press.

Editorial Research Reports
    1978   *The Rights Revolution.* Washington, D.C.: Congressional Quarterly, Inc.

Etzioni, Amitai
    1970   *Demonstration Democracy.* New York: Gordon and Breach.

Fine, Sidney
    1979   *Sit-down: The General Motors Strike of 1936-37.* Ann Arbor, Michigan: The University of Michigan Press.

Fink, Michael
    1980   "The Evolution of the American Protest Occupation: A Comparative Analysis." Unpublished paper, the University of California, Davis.

Garrow, David J.
    1978   *Protest at Selma: Martin Luther King, Jr. and the Voting Rights Act of 1965.* New Haven: Yale University Press.

Gitlin, Todd
    1980   *The Whole World Is Watching: Mass Media in the Making and Unmaking of the New Left.* Berkeley, CA.: University of California Press.

Heirich, Max
    1968   *The Spiral of Conflict: Berkeley 1964.* New York: Columbia University Press.

Lofland, John
    1981   "Collective Behavior: The Elementary Forms." Pp. 411-446
            in Morris Rosenberg and Ralph Turner (eds.) Social
            Psychology. New York: Basic Books.
Matthews, Donald R. and James Prothro
    1966   Negroes and the New Southern Politics.   New York:
            Harcourt, Brace and World.
Ornstein, Norman J. and Shirley Elder
    1978   Interest Groups, Lobbying and Policymaking. Washington,
            D.C.: Congressional Quarterly Press.
Piven, Francis Fox and Richard A. Cloward
    1977   Poor People's Movements: Why They Succeed, How They
            Fail. New York: Random House.
Salisbury, Robert
    1975   "Interest Groups."   Pp. 162-223 in F. Greenstein and
            N. Polsby (eds.), Non-Governmental Politics. Reading, MA.:
            Addison-Wesley.
Sharp, Gene
    1973   The Politics of Nonviolent Action. Boston: Porter Sargent.
Stiehm, Judith
    1972   Nonviolent Power. Lexington, MA.: D.C. Heath.
Taylor, Richard K.
    1977   Blockade: A Guide to Nonviolent Intervention. Maryknoll,
            N.Y.: Orbis Books.
Tilly, Charles
    1979   "Repertoires of Contention in America and Britain. 1750-
            1830." Pp. 125-155 in M. Zald and J. McCarthy (eds.) The
            Dynamics of Social Movements. Cambridge, MA.: Winthrop.
Turner, Ralph
    1970   "Determinants of Social Movement Strategies." Pp. 145-164
            in Tamotsu Shibutani (ed.), Human Nature and Collective
            Behavior. Englewood Cliffs, N.J.: Prentice-Hall.
Waskow, Arthur I.
    1966   From Race Riot to Sit-In, 1919 and the 1960s. Garden
            City, N.Y.: Anchor Books.
Zald, Mayer and J. D. McCarthy (eds.)
    1979   The Dynamics of Social Movements.   Cambridge, MA.:
            Winthrop.
Zinn, Howard
    1964   SNCC: The New Abolitionists. Boston: Beacon Press.

CHAPTER II

THE SYMBOLIC SIT-IN AND THE CALIFORNIA CAPITOL

It is against the background of the waves of protest occupation just reviewed that in the mid–seventies and early eighties a new form emerged, a form we called the "symbolic sit-in." The exact initiating episodes are difficult to determine but those taking place in the reception room of the Governor of California in late 1975 must likely be counted as among the pioneers.

A. FEATURES OF THE SYMBOLIC SIT-IN

(1) An initial and salient feature of the Capitol episodes is that they were called "sit-ins" or "occupations" by everyone, performers, media, authorities and others. That is, the imagery and language of "the-kind-of-event-this-is" was drawn directly from the not so long past history of protest occupations of the nineteen sixties. All parties used the terms "protest," "demands," "negotiation," "pressure" and other terms suggestive of protest as distinct from polite politics.

(2) The performers did, in fact, act in irregular ways; that is, ways that people in polite politics would not deign to act. At the mildest level of irregularity, picket signs were carried inside the Capitol and crowds paraded and stood about singing and chanting in the name of a demand. At its strongest, people slept overnight on the Governor's reception room floor, night after night, week after week and scurried about in raucously vocal crowds somewhat distracting Capitol workers from their ordinary tasks.

There are several features these episodes did not display that by their absence tell us some aspects that were present.

(3) Drawing from our previous discussion (Chapter I, section C), unlike classic protest occupations, standing patterns of activity at the Capitol were not disrupted significantly. Attention was accorded protesters, certainly, but nothing approaching the paralysis attendant to the sit-downs of industrial workers, the sit-ins of the civil righters, the sieges of students, or the bivouacs of anti-nuclearists.

Most took place in or were oriented to the Governor's reception room and an understanding of it and its microecological relation to the larger Capitol will help in understanding how these sit-ins were in effect encapsulated while still on display. The Governor's complex occupied a large portion of the ground floor of the Capitol building annex. Almost the entire south half of the interior space was sealed off in the sense that although there were five access doors, they were locked and unmarked. As such, the Governor and his immediate staff could not be approached by simply "walking in" or even barging in. Three of these five doors opened into a reception and waiting room twenty-four feet square and containing, most of the six year period, two couches, three chairs and tables, and the receptionist's desk and associated equipment. All three doors accessing the complex, one in each of the three walls adjoining the office complex, were ordinarily locked. Two of them were the routine modes of entrance and they were controlled by an electric lock system operated from behind the receptionist's desk. In such a fashion, the reception room was adjacent to the Governor and his people but quite carefully sealed off from them.

The wide fourth door of the room opened onto the broad main corridor of the Capitol Annex building and was across from the bank of elevators that ascended to the five legislative floors, the offices of the Senators, Assemblypersons, hearing rooms, and so forth. Traffic was heavy in this main corridor—thousands of persons came and went daily—and when the reception room doors were standing open—as they were during the day—anyone passing by the room could gaze in and see almost all of it at a glance. The room had, that is, a "fishbowl" quality: contained but thoroughly viewable. It was, indeed, a kind of public stage upon which actors might promenade but still not be terribly in anyone's way. This, then, was a site in which people could protest and be public and quite dramatic about their feelings without at the same time disrupting the ordinary flow of business.

These microecological aspects combined with a set of quasi-formal "rules for sitting-in" that the State Police had devised after the Governor responded to the initial reception room sleep-over declaration on November 20, 1975 by granting permission to do it. It is perhaps significant that the first sleep-inners were members of the United Farm Workers and personally led by the second most prominent person in that organization. The Governor was a long time and very active supporter of the UFW; another group might not have been treated so permissively.

Once having permitted the UFW, though, it was inconsistent then to deny sit-in "privileges" to subsequent protesters.

Be that as it may, State Police set the parameters and sit-inners largely operated within them. Even though disputed and renegotiated by both sides on occasion, the basic ones were no food in the reception room, no entrance after the building was locked at 10:00 p.m. (although one could leave), and little or no equipment beyond a sleeping bag. Further structuring the situation, a plainclothes policeman was on duty in the room around the clock (rotating in two hour shifts) and the bright fluorescent lights were left on all night.

(4) As the existence of "rules" implies, authorities treated the sit-ins as more or less routine matters rather than as a crisis and challenge. As we shall see in the accounts that follow, tempers sometimes "flared" on several sides, but these were momentary and soon curbed.

(5) Further unlike classic protest occupations, almost no "third parties" elected intensively to involve themselves in the episodes. No significant numbers of people either supportive of or hostile to the protesters appeared on the scene. Most often, no one paid much attention at all to them. Those who did were frequently just curious tourists and groups of school children who stared at the protesters rather in the way people look at strange animals in zoos. (For completeness sake, however, it needs to be reported that a small number of seemingly "media stimulated" "volunteers" did appear, especially at the longer symbolic sit-in episodes. Their participation was mostly short-lived and they were defined by sit-in leaders and others as "off the wall" and "kooky.")

The willingness of protesters to constrain their protest and to "play by the rules" combined with the willingness of authorities to allow mildly irregular, "symbolic" protest acts in technically trespassed official space provides, then, a new species, so to speak, of protest, the symbolic sit-in. Drawing forward the previous chapter's delineation of four levels of protest (symbolic, noncooperation, intervention and alternative institutions), the symbolic sit-in employs the rhetoric of true intervention but exercises the restraint of symbolic protest. In being restrained and in being permitted by authorities, however, it is fundamentally a form of symbolic rather than intervention protest.

The symbolic sit-in is in one sense an "evolved" form because it clearly takes its inspiration from, and is in part modeled on, intervention occupations of the sixties. But in another sense it is a regressive form because it also in some ways debases or dilutes the earlier meaning of the term "sit-in" and terms like it. The truly serious meanings and consequences associated with earlier sit-ins (and anti-nuclear bivouacs) are removed and that concept and associated terms come to mean only minor embarrassments and inconveniences on hard floors at a state capitol.

B.   TYPES OF SYMBOLIC SIT-INS AT THE CALIFORNIA CAPITOL

The some two dozen episodes of the symbolic sit-in we have selected for description and analysis in this report varied quite considerably among themselves. Perception of them as micro-protest entities is advanced if they are, in turn, divided in terms of their more conspicuous differences. Grouping them first in terms of what seem to be their global or "holistic" similarities, the episodes so clustered struck us as correlatively varying in terms of 1) duration, 2) size, and 3) level of what we will call "flex." The conjoining of the types with their characterizing variations is shown in Figure 1, "Types of Symbolic Sit-ins." Each of the types is explained in subsequent chapters and we therefore here only explicate the characterizing dimensions of variation.

(1)   "Total duration" refers to the elapsed clock time between the starting and ending of an episode. In terms of statistical frequency, most episodes only lasted a few minutes or hours. We report ten "pack-ins" (Chapter III) in order to illustrate subforms of them but several multiples of that number occurred over the six years under discussion. (Since no one kept records on them, the exact number is not known.) Slightly longer, about a dozen episodes, each, of "lone-ins" (Chapter IV) and "one night stands" (Chapter V) endured one to a few days. And just a little longer, two episodes of "spirited sieges" (Chapter VI) went several days. There is then a gap and a jump to staying overnight for weeks, a feat performed by three "long term vigils" (Chapter VII).

(2)   Sheer size is a significant difference, ranging from the lone protester up to, at some times, several hundred people. Within this, the larger scale and longer lasting episodes themselves varied considerably over time in the numbers making up their crowds. The general tendency was for their numbers to fall at night—often down to quite a token force—and to rise in the daytime, peaking at mid-day. And within these variations, the tendency was for total numbers displaying these variations to decline over the days and weeks.

(3)   There was intra-episode variation in what we might call "mobilization" or flex level. A low or "unflexed" level of mobilization involved people simply sitting about waiting for authorities to respond to them. In it, people read, chatted, or slept. Most symbolic sit-ins were at this level most of the time. Indeed, it must be reported that symbolic sit-ins were often quite boring and dull affairs.

Up slightly from this—a middle level—were group discussions and strategy sessions, interviews with media crews who came on the scene, and meetings with authorities. These served to punctuate time but were a relatively small portion of it. The highest level of mobilization seen among the episodes reported here consisted of marching, singing and chanting crowds and noisy debates with authorities in the presence of the full complement of sit-inners.

Figure 1

TYPES OF SYMBOLIC SIT-INS

		Variations		
		Total Duration	Size	Flex Level
Types	Pack-ins	hours	crowd	high
	Lone-ins	1 to several days	1 person	low
	One Night Stands	1-2 days	clique, small crowd	medium
	Spirited Sieges	days	crowd	medium to high
	Long Term Vigils	weeks	clique to crowd	low to medium

A sit-in can be characterized in terms of the degree to which it is dominantly oriented to one or another level of flex and we will do so in analyzing episodes in the chapters that follow.

Inspecting Figure 1, it can be seen that even confined to simple contrasts of three variables, each assuming only two or three states, a large number of major patterns are theoretically possible. This theoretical possibility of "randomly combined" features is of interest because those that actually occur are but a small subset from among this much larger and logical set of possibilities. The simplicity of the observed combinations suggests, in fact, a systemic quality, a strain toward consistency of features. Taking each type in turn, the pack-in is planned by its participants to be brief and it is thus under constraint to make its presence felt quickly. Quite rationally, the flex level needs to be high and can be high because the effort is quite short-term. Lone sit-inners are constrained by their very loneness not to be too "rowdy" lest they be defined as demented and taken into custody. Crowds get to sing, chant, and march about without casting significant doubt on their mental stability whereas loners are vulnerable to being defined as crazy or merely amusing; hence their reticence. (This is one of the more concrete and practical senses in which reality and sanity are functions of group action and support.)

The "one night stands" were typically clique or small crowd in size and somewhat assertive but much less so than the distinct pattern of the "spirited siege" in which (in full blown form), the flex level was as high as in pack-ins. (The two episodes of the spirited siege reported in Chapter VI were performed, however, by people otherwise defined as not especially dangerous—the blind, deaf and the developmentally disabled—who derived a certain "license to flex" from their less than full competencies. Moreover, their sit-ins were of a few days duration and had more or less predetermined and known termination dates.)

In contrast, the longer term vigils embued their efforts with an aura of restraint. In vowing to stay an indeterminant period of time, they could ill-afford too spirited a siege. Further, the movements mounting two of the three episodes were reputationally associated with violence (The United Farm Workers) or civil disobedience (the anti-nuclear movement), features doubtless counseling special caution.

C. CHRONOLOGY OF MAJOR EPISODES

Grouping symbolic sit-ins in terms of their microsocial patterns heightens analytic appreciation but it also violates their historical sequence. One consequence of violating temporal order is an obscuring of ways in which there may have been an evolution of types of episodes and ways in which earlier episodes provided models for later ones. For purposes of addressing these and other questions, we provide a chronology of all the episodes that involved staying overnight in the Governor's reception room (or at the ALRB office in Office Building Number One) as a protest action.

Nineteen Seventy-Five

November 20-24, four nights (Thursday...Monday): About sixty members of the United Farm Workers demand changes in the operation of the Agricultural Labor Relations Board.

December 3-4, one night (Wednesday): About thirty-five wives of medical doctors, and others, demand a special session of the Legislature on medical malpractice insurance reform.

December 12-13, one night (Friday): About fifteen parents of institutionalized and developmentally disabled children demand better treatment of their offspring in state hospitals.

Nineteen Seventy-Six

January 12-28, fourteen nights (Monday...Wednesday): A physician demands reform in malpractice insurance.

January 19-20, one night (Wednesday): A woman, aged 72, protests curtailment of a federally sponsored and state administered escort service for senior citizens.

June 29-July 29, twenty-nine nights (Tuesday...Thursday): Groups varying from about five to thirty members of the Network Against Psychiatric Assault (NAPA) demand minimum wages for mental hospital patients who work and they protest "various hospital practices such as electroshock and use of certain drugs" (Sacramento Bee, 1976).

Nineteen Seventy-Seven

March 2-16, fifteen nights (Wednesday...Wednesday): Farmworkers and their supporters varying in number from a token two or three to over two hundred demand that the ALRB ban alleged company unions from bargaining agent elections and protest certain actions of that agency's general counsel. The sleep-in activities are conducted at the ALRB offices and, for a period, delegations are deployed daily to the Governor's reception room.

April 27-29, two nights (Wednesday...Friday): Four farm worker families (about twenty-five people) demand access to labor camp housing. They sleep one night in the reception room and one night in the conference room of the Secretary of Health and Welfare (at the invitation of the Secretary).

June 22-24, two nights (Wednesday...Friday): An initial group of about forty deaf and blind people and their supporters demand continuation of a Client Assistance Program that is scheduled for termination June 30.

June 27-July 1, four nights (Wednesday...Saturday): Crowds sometimes as large as 300 and groups sometimes as small as a dozen demand no cuts in the funding of day care centers for the developmentally handicapped. The larger crowds are predominately such disabled adults. The smaller ones are about evenly divided between them and their staff caretakers.

July 28, one night (Thursday): A middle-aged mother and her teenage, developmentally handicapped son protest conditions in the state hospital for the disabled in which her son is a patient.

Nineteen Seventy-Eight

March 13-22 (estimated), three sporadic nights: Groups varying from two to a dozen members of the Gray Panthers protest the planned closing of a state-funded nursing facility for senior citizens.

Nineteen Seventy-Nine

November 28-January 2 (1980), thirty-seven nights (Wednesday...Friday): A group varying between about 200 and half a dozen demand the Governor close a nuclear power plant near the Capitol.

Nineteen Eighty

February 12-13, one night (Tuesday): Three members of the anti-nuclear protest, just above, resume their overnight presence.

March 29-30, one night (Friday): Six anti-nuclear protesters sleep over one night commemorating the first anniversary of the near-disaster at the Three Mile Island nuclear plant.

In trend terms, we have this sequence:

1975:	3
1976:	3
1977:	5
1978:	1
1979:	1
1980:	2

The numbers are small but they display the classic "collective behavior curve" of a relatively rapid rise to a peak followed by more rapid fall-off and a final "blip", a curve also found in the occurrence of ghetto riots, student protests, and lifestyle fashions and fads (Penrose, 1952; Irwin, 1977; Spilerman, 1976).

The quite distinctive skewing of the social categories of persons electing to sleep-in also merits notation. Only two approach being a "mainstream" or establishment "social types" of persons, the doctors' wives and the physician. Even here it is significant that these are the doctor's wives and that the lone doctor was a black male who practiced in the Watts area of Los Angeles. Three episodes involved farm workers, a troubled and marginal occupation by all accounts and one in turmoil for many years in California. Three additional episodes were mounted by the underemployed "intellectual proletariat" (the anti-nuclearists) (Widmer et al., 1979). Seven, almost half, were performed by traditionally stigmatized groups that have begun in recent times to develop a political voice: mental patients, the aged, the deaf and blind, and the developmentally handicapped.

D. SOCIAL REACTION

One important question about sit-ins is, of course, what are their effects, or at least, how do people react to them? In order best to answer this question in relation to those observed at the California Capitol, we need to specify elements in terms of which there can be a reaction. A first distinction is in terms of audiences. Sitting-in was an act designed to draw the attention of media and officials. Ideally, one got the attention of both and that attention had a mutually reinforcing effect: the attention of one made the other take the protesters more seriously. Second, the attention drawn can itself be divided into reaction to the "cause" or objectives as distinct from the tactic of sitting in itself. Considered conjointly, there are, thus, four basic clusters of social reaction.

(1) Official reaction to the goals or objectives of sit-ins occupy us in the main chapters and in the conclusion. We therefore postpone its discussion.

(2) Media reaction to the objectives of the sit-ins may be characterized as "positive" in the sense that what seemed an ordinary portion of the Capitol press corps would typically appear, collect material, and present it in words and pictures. We say "ordinary portion" in order to point up that very few "stories" at the Capitol drew anything near half of the press corps. The run of the mill Capitol news conference staged in the Capitol press conference room (Room 1190), a citadel of polite politics, might draw on the order of a dozen media teams/persons and sit-ins seem to have about the same attention-gaining potential. Nonetheless, that was no mean feat; one was likely to get media attention, billed as a sit-in, complete with an interesting picture.

(3 and 4) Distinct from these are questions of reactions to sitting in per se, irrespective of the objectives of sitting-in. As seen in the sleep-in chronology, above, protest occupations started November 20, 1975

and there were three episodes in quick succession. The Sacramento Bee responded to them in early December of that year with a "lets make light of it" feature headlined "Check Yer Arms [:] The Fight to Sleep in [The Governor's...] Office" (Lewis, 1975). Tongue in cheek, the writer compared the accommodations to a hotel, noting it accepts no reservations, has only one room and is not listed in Michelin. Calling it the "Governor's Inn," the bathroom facilities were rated as "no more convenient than those at a third-rate rooming house."

Into January, 1976, the Los Angeles Times opened a story on the phenomenon with the declaration: "It is in the best American tradition to petition your government, but this is getting ridiculous!" (Endicott, 1976). Obliquely referring to "pack-ins" (Chapter III, below) the story described demonstrators "literally shoulder to shoulder" and the reception room as a "madhouse." "A television cameraman climbed on [the receptionist's] ...desk to get a better shot of the crowd...." It was a "...giant media event running out of control," because several demonstrating groups were on the scene simultaneously and pressing their case by packing into the reception room (Endicott, 1976).

The mid-1976 long term vigil of NAPA (Network Against Psychiatric Assault) provoked the ire of a State Senator who said, for the media, that he was "absolutely outraged by the stench arising from the dirty, disheveled reception room" (Sacramento Bee, 1976). In a letter to the State Health director that he made public, the Senator requested an investigation into the "health and safety" aspects. Several days later a Sacramento Union columnist characterized the reception room as a "pig sty," claiming that visitors were "appalled at the degradation" and he called for an end to using the room as a "public camp ground" (Waters, 1976).

Over the labor day weekend of 1976, the carpet of the reception room was replaced with a hardwood floor, an event itself an object of Sacramento Bee reporting under the headline "Governor's Office takes a Hard Look." The reporter interpreted the change as an effort to discourage sleep-ins without banishing them and characterized the office as having been the "scene of numerous demonstrations" (Skelton, 1976).

As shown in the chronology, above, there was a lull in late 1976 and early 1977, but a "spurt" in mid-1977 that was accompanied by an upsurge in rallies, pickets and pack-ins more generally. This moved the editors of the Sacramento Bee to editorialize July 1, 1977. Under the declaration "End the Sit-ins," the unsigned statement claimed "the mass sit-ins and, at times, sleep-ins are no way to air an alleged injustice." The Governor has been "overly tolerant" with groups "besieging the reception area of the governor's office" and if he will not speak out against them, "we will: the inside demonstrations are becoming a nuisance and should be curtailed before they develop into a destructive tradition" (Sacramento Bee, 1977).

As it happened, the incidence of such events declined without official action and there was also little more social reaction until late 1979 when the anti-nuclear demonstrators occupied the room for thirty-eight days. Early in January, 1980, the two upholstered (and decrepit) couches and four cushioned chairs were replaced with hard, wooden benches and matching coffee tables. These were dutifully pictured in the media together with text that drew explicit attention to how this change made life more difficult for prospective sit-inners (Sacramento Bee, 1980; Sacramento Union, 1980). Seeing them in the reception room for the first time, the Governor was quoted as commenting "this looks bleak" (Associated Press, 1980).

In addition, over time the State Police "rules" of protest occupations grew slowly more restrictive. Earlier occupiers ate in the reception room, used sleeping bags, and the twenty-nine night NAPA protest of 1976 even had mattresses. In 1977, the State Police were attempting to prohibit all such accoutrements, albeit the Title XX coalition negotiated more supplies on the grounds of having special, physical needs (see Chapter VI).

Taking the themes appearing in the media together with impressions we have formed from conversations with the variously involved, it can perhaps be said that the major reaction to sit-ins was bemused humor and curiosity. Obviously and as also reported, a few people were clearly irked and disapproving. But it is our sense that this was far from the dominant reaction which was much more benign or even supportive. Several aspects of the sequence of protests (that also serve to elaborate our prior depiction of the symbolic sit-in) make this dominant reaction more understandable. First, there was rarely, if ever, any problem of actual violence or even threat of violence. Many groups sang and chanted but such acts were not defined as presaging "stronger" measures. Second, the "causes" espoused by the various groups were all ones for which there was reasonably widespread public sympathy, support, or indifference. None of the groups promoted "radical" or otherwise unpopular political (or religious) enterprises. Third, the Governor of California seemed to us to be surprisingly important as a reference point for people in deciding how they ought to feel about the activities in the reception room (and a wide range of other matters). During the period in question he obviously "allowed" the protests. In the same period, it needs also to be known, he was quite frequently criticized for failing to take positions on a great many matters; that is, people wanted to know how "the Governor felt" and to take that into account in developing their own views. The fact that he even sometimes met with sit-inners (and his staff frequently did) provided them a more than ordinary sort of legitimacy—or at least defined them as benign.

As mentioned, we will take up questions of the policy effects or "success" of sit-ins in the last chapter.

E. DATA AND METHOD

The data we report are drawn from a variety of sources spanning several years. The first author directly observed almost all the events occurring in 1977. These include most of the "pack-ins" reported in Chapter III, the spirited sieges of Chapter VI and the long term vigil of the United Farm Workers treated in Chapter VII. The second author developed the historical materials and observed the anti-nuclear protest analyzed in Chapter VII. Description of these and other episodes were supplemented by interviewing participants and officials. Events earlier than 1977 are largely reconstructed from newspaper accounts and interviews with selected officials. The distance in time, the scattering of participants, and the limits of our resources made us decide not to undertake detailed reconstruction of the earliest episodes—those occurring in 1975 and 1976. We do provide sketches of their basic features but not of their more intimate dynamics, the kind of detail that requires intensive and direct observation at the time of the event.

Our method was relatively standard fieldwork of the sort well known in social science. The first author was known to leading participants as a sociologist studying "crowds in politics." Often, though, in the briefer episodes, he simply blended in with the Capitol press corps from which he did not differentiate himself. The second author began observation as a sit-inner and "unknown observer" but toward the end of the PUARS vigil reported his interest in writing it up to several leaders who cooperated with further interviews.

While we were observers of episodes, we were not "insiders" to any. Each had a central "clique" of some sort that either had pre-existing solidarity or developed it through decision-making action on the scene. We were not part of any such circles and one limitation of our accounts is lack of, or only second-hand access to, the more intimate and secret exchanges among leaders. Moreover, in many cases it was difficult to do post sit-in interviews in which we could have faith. Even though these were "only" symbolic sit-ins, there was nonetheless a good deal of wariness of outsiders and a concern to make only an appropriate impression for the good of the "cause." But despite these limits, the results of leader deliberations were apparent in subsequent actions and the at least public reckoning of what went into decisions was available.

For several reasons, we have elected not to identify individuals by their actual names, including even officials such as the Governor. Mainly, we hope to foster attention to forms and processes and to avoid bogging down in the idiosyncrasies of personalities. However, we do use the real names of organizations and we have not changed any of the actual dates and places.

NOTE

1.   The following were among the quieter of such outside "volunteers." The deaf/blind "spirited siege" analyzed in Chapter VI drew three piggybackers: an elderly crippled man with barely coherent complaints about his disability payments; a woman quietly alleging to individual sit-inners the existence of a mafia-federal government conspiracy to disable Americans with a gas disguised as cigarette smoke; a similarly discrete woman counseling that all problems could be solved if one were in tune with nature.   The four-day spirited siege of the Title XX coalition (also discussed in Chapter VI) picked up two multi-day piggybackers, one of whom, an unemployed heavy equipment operator in his forties, carried a brief case containing a sheaf of his own and other letters dealing with the large number of his conflicts with merchants, police, judges, doctors and others over service improperly rendered, especially to his car, his driving, harassment by various policemen, and debates about his exact physical condition.   He tended to arrive at the reception room in the afternoon, to ask the receptionist to see the Governor, and to be told that the Governor was busy but that he could wait or see someone else in the Governor's office.   He would elect to wait and then sit about amidst the sit-inners crowding the room, quietly starting conversation with the "normals" present and slowly drawing them into his very elaborate catalog of woes and displays of correspondence pertinent to those troubles.

More vocal and raucous outsiders included a disorganized person the State Police took into medical custody, at the Title XX Coalition episode, and one verbal attacker, each, at the farm worker pack-in reported in Chapter III and the Three Mile Island Memorial Sit-in reported in Chapter V.

REFERENCES

Associated Press
        1980   "Governor's Visitors Won't Rest Easily."   San Francisco Chronicle, February 12.
Endicott, William
        1976   "Hundred Jam Capitol, Push Causes: Protesters Range from Farm Workers to Doctors." Los Angeles Times, January 1.
Irwin, John
        1977   Scenes. Beverly Hills: Sage.
Lewis, Jim
        1975   "Check-Yer Arms: They Fight to Sleep in [The Governor's]...Office." Sacramento Bee, December 6.
Penrose, L. S.
        1952   On the Objective Study of Crowd Behavior.   London: H. K. Lewis.

26   SYMBOLIC SIT-INS

Sacramento Bee
    1976   "[Governor's]...Office Sit-in Angers Modesto Lawmaker."
          July 20.
    1977   "End the Sit-ins."   July 1.
    1980   "Hard Times for Protesters."   February 13.
Sacramento Union
    1980   "Governor's Benches 'More Appropriate.'"   February 12.
Skelton, Nancy
    1976   "Sleep-in Protests: Governor's Office Takes a Hard Look."
          Sacramento Bee, September 8.
Spilerman, Seymour
    1976   "Structural Characteristics of Cities and the Severity of
          Racial Disorders."   *American Sociological Review* 41:771-
          793.
Waters, Earl G.
    1976   "[Governor's] Office Looks Like a Camp Ground."   *The
          Davis Enterprise*, July 30.
Widmer, George et al.
    1979   *Strange Victories: The Anti-nuclear Movement in the U.S.
          and Europe.*   Brooklyn, N.Y.: Midnight Notes Collective.

CHAPTER III

PACK-INS

As a micro-form of protest, the pack-in has these earmarks:

1)   the acting unit is a "crowd" (acknowledging a degree of ambiquity about how many people are required in order to make a crowd);

2)   the leaders and members of the crowd act in what is conventionally defined as an impolite, irregular and improperly ostentatious manner;

3)   such behavior is employed in making demands to officials in the officials' place of work;

4)   the event lasts a few hours, at most.

In this chapter we focus on the special form of the pack-in that had the peculiarity of being directed to the Governor's office or, more precisely, his reception room. It is helpful to recognize, though, that milder versions of the practice were sometimes also directed to other targets in the arena of the California Capitol. Most conspicuous among them are what has been termed "emergency crowd swarms," a pattern in which dozens to a few thousand members of an interest group appeared at the Capitol in order virtually to deluge the offices of legislators with delegations supporting or opposing pieces of legislation (Lofland, 1982: Chapter 3). Most were distinct from pack-ins by virtue of their restraint but they were like pack-ins in using crowds that appeared in officials' places of work and by their sheer scale tending to disrupt the ordinary flow of business.

A. RALLY TO PACK-IN SEQUENCES

The most dramatic form of the pack-in was composed of two main on-the-scene phases. The centerpiece of the first phase was a late morning or noon-time outdoor rally near the main Capitol entrance addressed by a series of group leaders and supporters. Two of four such sequences observed in 1977 prefaced their rally by marching in a circle in the rally area while chanting and carrying picket signs. Members of the other two simply stood about as their numbers arrived and they "began" the rally. The speeches of declarations, demands, and supports served publicly to define the situation of assembly and became the direct step-off point from which leaders directed their respective crowds to move inside the Capitol building in order to "visit the Governor." Given that the Governor's reception room was only twenty-four by twenty-four feet square, even relatively small crowds—twenty or so persons—could appear to be packing it, especially if the members were holding large picket signs or carrying one or more cloth banners or flags held open by two persons.

Approaching the receptionist, a leader would ask to see the Governor, almost invariably, without having an appointment. Informed that he was busy, the requesters would be told that they were welcome to wait for him and perhaps to see an aide. The propensity was to demand the Governor nonetheless. This almost ritual demand-refusal-demand exchange initiated a vocal protest phase. One such, observed in February of 1977, was engaged in by some seventy ethnic minority mothers and their children who were led by several young, Anglo and middle class females and males. In order to protest certain proposed cuts in child care centers, they had come from San Francisco by bus, arriving in the late morning. Picketing the Department of Education building and rallying outside Office Building Number One, they entered the Capitol, chanting, at noon and formed a semi-circle in the reception room and chanted:

No on 5, Keep Child Care Alive

*   *   *

We Want [the first name of the then Governor]

One of their Anglo male leaders, in "leftist-college-scruffy" garb, shouted comments on the reception room posters that promoted a "save the whale" campaign of the Governor, declaring that the Governor cared more about whales than children (one picket sign alleged that the Governor ignored children because he had none of his own). The chanting endured some ten minutes, the crowd filed out, dispersed on benches in Capitol Park and had their box lunches.

Rather more assertive were the some one hundred Chicano cannery workers who in late July of 1977 rallied on the North Capitol lawn in order to call attention to alleged discrimination and other abuses in canneries and the failure of the Teamsters union and cannery owners to act appropriately. Listening to speeches between 11:30 a.m. and 12:30 p.m. the crowd paraded into the Capitol and crammed into the reception room. Unable to see the Governor, organizers led chanting and singing, especially in the presence of television crews who, exiting the Capitol for lunch, happened on to the group.

Time passed and their numbers began to decline: 60 at 1:00 p.m.; 40 at 2:00 p.m.   What had started out as an enthusiastic, singing and chanting crowd became a grimly quiet and increasingly despondent gathering, especially as the temperature in the room rose because body heat was overcoming the cooling system.   Finally, after 2:00 p.m., the leader snapped at the receptionist "Tell the Governor, thanks for nothing." Shortly, he and the last of the dwindling crowd simply left.

A still more assertive level of pack-in was mounted as a response to the riotous end of a Northern California cause celebre.   In early August of 1977 a nine year struggle to "save the International Hotel" in San Francisco ended with police on horseback attacking a thousand demonstrators massed to prevent the eviction of 45 elderly, mostly Filipino and Chinese, residents who themselves went limp and had to be carried out.   The next day, at noon, thirty youth, largely Asian, in denim-left student dress, assembled on the North Capitol lawn and formed into a chanting, revolving ring.   Carrying picket signs and posting an eight foot banner declaring "Stop Attacks on Third World Working Peoples' Communities," their chants included "Support the I Hotel/Reverse the Evictions Now."   Interspersed with that chant, specific to the occasion, was the all-purpose left wing chant of the time:

THE PEO-PLE/U-NI-TED/WILL NE-VER BE DE-FEAT-ED
THE PEO-PLE/U-NI-TED/WILL NE-VER BE DE-FEAT-ED

At about 12:30, a leader announced over his hand-held PA system: "OK, let's rally now."   The small crowd sat down in a huddle to listen to representatives of several local young-person, left-wing groups, including a tenant's association, The Friends of China, and a not-so-left association of Asian state employees.

The second phase commenced at 12:50 p.m. with a form-up to proceed to the Governor's reception room.   Chanting on the move and in the reception room, the crowd formed a circle around the walls and furniture of the room and held up their signs.   A leader requested an audience with the Governor or an aide.   Neither was reported available. Action thus stalled, the decision was made to proceed to the office of the Lt. Governor which was just down the hall.   All tried to enter the Lt. Governor's reception room but due to smallness, it soon became packed with ten or so people still crowding to get through the door. An aide appeared and announced that she could see two or so of them in her office but not the entire group. The leaders refused to send a delegation (a common tack in the "confrontational" style) and asked that a conference room large enough to hold all of them be found. The aide promised to do so and to report her success or not in one hour. This also was refused by the crowd: the meeting had to be now and the leaders suggested they reassemble outside on the North lawn, which the aide accepted. In this exchange, the aide made repeated note that the protesters had not given advance notice of their appearance or made an appointment with anyone, thereby making it difficult to grant their meeting request on the spot. (We see in this, of course, the micro-politics of power, of who is willing to wait on whom. These and other demonstrators were not willing either to make advance appointments or to wait long for officials on occasions of surprise visits. To have done so would have been to grant officials deference and power the demonstrators did not feel was owed to them.)

Reassembled, sitting in a bunch on the lawn before the aide who was also seated on the lawn, the leaders presented their demands that the I hotel tenants be returned to the hotel and that the Lt. Governor make a public commitment of his support within one week. The aide listened, took notes, and maintained that she could not promise a reply within one week much less a promise of support. There were several exchanges on this issue and finally the aide, a young black woman, left amicably. Several of the leaders then lectured the others on how this had been the typical behavior of politicians and none of them could be trusted. The only alternative was for people to take "direct responsibility" for their lives and develop "mass support," such as they had done there today. They had only even been talked to that day because they had a demonstration; appointments were not necessary. The second period on the north lawn had lasted about half an hour, from 1:00 to 1:30 p.m., and after these admonitions, participants drifted off in cliques of two, three and four.

The most zealous and long-lived of pack-ins observed consisted of about one hundred Chicano farm workers and their Anglo organizers protesting the worker displacement consequences of farm mechanization. Assembled the late morning of a day in September, 1977, they heard several short speeches—almost all in Spanish—before moving, at noon, into the reception room. Too many for the room, some thirty overflowed into the main Capitol corridor. Told they could wait on the likelihood of seeing the Governor, a guitar playing Anglo organizer led the crowd in numerous songs, many taken from the song booklet with which each person was supplied. Mostly in Spanish, the songs included "We Shall Overcome," "We Shall Not be Moved," and "Whose Side Are You On?" A chant of "Machines No, Work Yes" (in Spanish), among other chants, interspersed singing. Shouting at the top of his voice and interrupted by frequent yells and claps of approval, the leader read out their demands.

These included an end to farm mechanization research until its effects were documented, retraining programs for displaced farmworkers, farmworker housing, resettlement on publicly owned farmland and emergency financial assistance.

About 12:30, the some twenty-five children in their ranks were taken outside by several adults. Over the first two hours, television crews came upon them as they were exiting the Capitol and elected to interview the leaders. Each time portions of the crowd assembled behind the leader and burst into a new wave of zealous singing and waving of picket signs. Their signs were quite professionally done and colorful, making impressive media poses that were particularly attractive to television crews.

Close to 1:00 p.m., sandwiches were passed out. Into the afternoon, there were seemingly endless rounds of clapping, chanting and singing led by the guitar playing organizer. About 1:30, the twenty-five children returned, invigorating the chanting, singing and clapping.

At 1:45 the first of what would be a series of four officials who supported them appeared and spoke encouragement to the crowd. The first was the director of the Department of Health, a medical doctor about whom people frequently mentioned that he had once been the personal physician of the almost sainted head of the United Farm Workers. Shortly after he left, there was an unusual episode revolving around one of the Capitol "characters," a woman known only as "Virginia." In her mid-fifties and standing perhaps five feet tall, she was a "Capitol regular" in that she was seen lounging at the Capitol on most days although she was not there on any political or other official business. She observed many rallies and was ordinarily quiet but this day she loudly and aggressively denounced this crowd and its leader, telling him to shut up and that their presence was a waste of time. Organizers tried to escort her out but she resisted. Only after considerable placation did she stop speaking and suddenly withdraw. (This event was notable because of its extreme rarity. "Baiting" of this or any other sort was virtually never seen at Capitol protests.)

At 2:00 p.m. an aide to the Secretary of Health and Welfare arrived and addressed the crowd, followed by a State Senator who promised his support and enjoined them to wait for the Governor. After he left the crowd chanted "We want [the Governor's last name]." A lull ensued. The children were growing restless. Gradually adults and children began to leave and by 3:30 some 50 people remained. Many of them were sitting in the hall or strolling in the park just outside the building.

The aide who had spoken previously reappeared just after 3:30, announcing that he had learned the Governor would be in town until 8:00 p.m. at which time he was leaving for Canada. Those now remaining decided they would continue to wait and some went out for food and coffee.

Toward 4:00 p.m. uniformed policemen were seen in the halls more frequently and at 4:30 a plainclothes member of the Governor's security force came into the reception room and announced to the some half a dozen people there at that moment that eating and drinking were not permitted.   And, if they planned to stay overnight, sleeping bags were not allowed.   Down to about forty people toward 5:00 p.m., the scene was quiet with most of the young, Anglo organizers and Chicano women in the reception room and the Chicano males gathered in the hall, around the leader.

Time wore on and the Governor finally emerged and spoke with them briefly just after 7:00 p.m. and he agreed to meet with a small delegation of them at a later time. The Secretary of Health and Welfare also spoke with them at this time and was charged by the Governor to arrange a meeting. Satisfied, the group left.

B. PACK-IN TO HEARING MAU-MAU SEQUENCES

A second pattern of pack-in posturing was more clearly linked to quite immediate political decisions at the Capitol.   The crowd would have arrived in order to attend a hearing scheduled that day and a reception room pack-in was in addition to appearance at a hearing.

But appearance at a hearing was not merely a presence; in this pattern it was a "mau-mau" presence, to use Tom Wolfe's (1971) term for the crowd practice of acting in an aggressive manner toward officials. Two instances of this pattern can be reported.   In the first, about 50 developmentally disabled adults and their caretakers assembled at noon on the North lawn one day in April, 1977. Planning to testify before an Assembly subcommittee appropriation hearing that afternoon, the caretakers aimed first to make their situation public by bringing officials face-to-face with some of the physically and mentally handicapped people about whom they were making decisions. Two senators and other officials stopped and talked briefly with leaders but also desiring the attention of the Governor, the crowd was moved by caretakers to his reception room and led in chanting "We Won't Go Back," the issue being the fate of an 18.9 million dollar augmentation to keep recreation—day care— centers open. If the augmentation failed, many clients would have to return to institutions, it was asserted. After a few minutes of chanting, the nattily suited and hat-wearing Secretary of Health and Welfare appeared, together with his equally well outfitted entourage (including a massive plainclothes State Policeman). As we have already seen, crowd noise and TV cameras at high noon in the Governor's reception room did not guarantee the appearance of high government officials, but it seemed sometimes to help, as in this case, and, at the request of officials, the caretakers moved their charges back to the North lawn.

Several television crews and radio people filmed and recorded the sad tales told by the handicapped about their imminent loss of recreational and other opportunities. Although members of this crowd lacked picket signs, they drew the prolonged and curious stares of the lunchtime parade of Capitol workers and other regulars because many of them dressed in a manner and had physical appearances quite visibly out of the ordinary, as well as displaying unusual bits of speech and behavior. Several wheelchairs were also visible. All of this was, in its way, the functional equivalent of picket signs.

Officials and media departed before 1:00 p.m. and there was a lull until just past 2:00 when most of the group moved to the small hearing room where testimony on the appropriation was to be heard. Taking almost all of the available seats, some forty members of the crowd signed up to testify. Arriving and viewing the rather unusual audience, the subcommittee chair spoke and conducted the hearing with studied forebearance and permissiveness. For, the crowd cheered, yelled and clapped hands before and after each testifier, punctuating their sounds with cries of "right on" and "shove it to them." No officials admonished them—a rather unusual occurrence at Capitol hearings where audiences were ordinarily quiet and incipient boisterousness was halted by presiding and other officials and order was enforced by a Sergeant-at-arms corps. Further, some testifiers threatened to "spank" and otherwise to punish members of the Committee if the money was not forthcoming. One vowed to have the Governor's father spank him should he veto the appropriation, an idea some of the Members appeared to find humorous. Another, toward the end of what I personally found to be a grotesque procession, spoke only in groans and moans; others spoke in inaudibly soft tones; still others were incoherent. But, through it all, the "normals" acted as if nothing was amiss; that is, the handicapped were indulged, a response observed in other situations in which the speakers are defined as somehow less than competent persons but not incompetent in a way that was physically or socially threatening. In addition, caretakers and parents were sprinkled through the string of mentally retarded speakers, thus communicating that there was some control on the scene.

At the end, the Chair said, "We are all very proud of you because you had the courage to come and speak." However, the Committee would not vote on the 18.9 million that day owing to the need to consider "all the needs." Murmurs of dissatisfaction went up and timid voices of protest were heard but the agenda moved to the next item. The caretakers moved their charges out of the hearing room and some hallway indecision ensued: a vote had been expected. One leader wanted again to chant and protest in the Governor's reception room—as they had done before the hearing—but others said no. It was then about 3:30 p.m. and the practical problems of coping with the handicapped and getting them back to San Francisco, from where they had all come in several specially outfitted vans, were looming up. Retreat won out. The vans were brought up onto the Capitol sidewalks and the staff loaded up their charges. (This small and chanting confrontation was but prelude. Some of them would almost literally take up residence in the Governor's reception room at the end of June, an episode described in Chapter VI.)

A second episode of hearing mau-mau linked to a pack-in was fielded by the some seven hundred "Family Farmers" who converged on the Convention Center in a virtual fleet of chartered Greyhound buses the morning of November 7, 1977. Armed with abundant, hand-made and lettered picket signs, American flags, and with "No on 160" and "We are Family Farmers" stick-on patches and buttons affixed to their clothes, they picketed before the convention center auditorium a brief time. Their signs expressed sentiments such as:

160 Acres of Unreality

*   *   *

Stop Socialistic Agrarian Experiments

*   *   *

It's Our Land, No Free Rides

*   *   *

Agrarian Reformers Get a Job

They then filed into the 1,000 seat auditorium where officials of the Department of Interior were holding hearings on Federally funded irrigation in relation to limits on family farm ownership of land. Filling in the back sector of the auditorium, they held up their signs toward the hearing panel and applauded and waved signs for each testifier they liked.

At noon, hundreds of boxes of chicken from the fast food chain featuring a Kentucky Colonel were distributed among them as they lounged in groups outdoors on the landscape of the Convention Center. Shortly past 12:30, the male leader said merely "let's go" and the crowd began to form up several abreast in clusters, moving toward the Capitol. Fully extended, the procession was more than two blocks long and filled the sidewalks. The front clusters had entered the Capitol north doors and begun to crowd into the Governor's reception room when the State Police stopped the middle and rear of the line at the doors with the order that picket signs with handles were not allowed inside the Capitol. Unknowledgeable that this was not quite the law, and with their leaders already talking to the Governor's receptionist, these good middle class citizens milled about and put their signs down beside the door. This disruption effectively disorganized the flow of their parade. Many began to examine the wonders of the ground-floor corridor of the Capitol building, especially the county display boxes built into the walls.

In the reception room, leaders approached the Governor's receptionist and asked to see that august person. Allowing that they had not made an appointment, they were told he was not available but that they could wait or leave him a message. They elected to leave a message, the forever unflappable receptionist calmly and carefully writing down that 700 family farmers had stopped by to see the Governor. Indeed, she scrupulously acquired even more details than the leaders offered. (One was reminded of comedian Bob Newhart's King Kong routine in which the night watchman of the Empire State Building cautiously phones his superior for advice on what to do about the ape climbing the building. In both cases, there was an effort to treat more or less bizarre events as routine matters. Consider, too, how many people can return to their offices and read the message that 700 family farmers had dropped by to see them?!)

This parade-through was not a matter of advance knowledge to the State Police—unlike many other large-crowd display events—and one indicator of police surprise was the large number of them (ten were counted) that suddenly appeared in the corridors—plainclothes and uniformed officers alike. This was in contrast to the more ordinary practice of deploying one or two uniformed persons for a brief period except where crowds were involved in crossing streets and traffic control became a consideration—a problem that did not arise inside the Capitol.

After some more hesitant milling the crowd moved in clusters, but still relatively parade-like, back to the convention center where they again picketed briefly and then resumed their audience role at the hearing. Shortly before 2:00 p.m., they exited the hearing en masse, an event difficult not to notice since it left the large auditorium virtually empty, and boarded their fleet of buses for home—diverse points in the great Central Valley of California.

C. CONVENTION TO PACK-IN SEQUENCES

The pack-ins just discussed were planned components of a round of activities at the Capitol. In contrast, a few were more emergent and connected, further, with two or more day conventions or conferences being conducted physically close to the Capitol. One occurring in June of 1979 rose out of a "First Summit of Black Concerns" attended by "more than 2,000" prominent black leaders "from throughout the nation" (Maganini, 1979). About two hundred of them organized a rally at the Capitol and a "slogan chanting march on the Governor's office" emerged from it (Assagai, 1979a). "After the marchers sang civil rights songs and demanded a conference with [...the Governor]," the governor's office agreed to a face-to-face meeting with representatives of the group. Sacramento <u>Bee</u> reporter Mel Assagai (1979b) observed of the episode that their "angry voices, civil rights songs and confrontation tactics made for a dramatic moment" and "transformed what could have been just another conference...into a force to be reckoned with."

This effort was in that way much more successful than the one emerging from the convention of the California Service Station Association who on August 31, 1979 "squeezed into [the Governor's] ...outer office and spilled into nearby Capitol corridors," demanding the Governor's appearance, which they did not get (McBride, 1979). They did provide, though, the nice touch of littering the receptionist's desk with their business cards, a kind of printed roll call of many who had been present.

D. PROTEST THREATS

Two other types of crowd actions were not precisely pack-ins but were closely enough related to warrant description in this context. One of them was an emergency convened press conference that carried with it the <u>threat</u> of a protest occupation in order to get the attention of officials. It was staged by some twenty-five members and supporters of the United Farm Workers, midday, Friday, June 3, 1977. Engaged in organizing workers at a farm some fifty miles from the Capitol, on June 2 a "private security" guard struck down a UFW organizer in the presence of local police who despite witnessing the assault insisted that it did not occur, UFW people claimed. Distressed that authorities thus communicated that they were not going to punish and thereby deter further violence, the UFW organizer at the scene decided to appeal to the Agricultural Labor Relations Board (ALRB) for protection, an organization headquartered on the third floor of Office Building Number One, a structure across the street from the Capitol. Appearing in a group of about thirty the next day, media had been notified and were on the scene, filming the crowd formed up around a several foot square red, white and black UFW flag. Hand-held, red UFW banners were visible along with a few picket signs. In successive media interviews, the spokesperson announced that the workers intended to stay there as long as necessary to get assurances of protection from the ALRB. Close to noon, sandwiches and a fruit-flavored drink were brought in by UFW staff (the union maintained a multi-person lobby office near the Capitol). After eating, the small crowd caucused, decided their point had already been made, and left the premises.

A rally-centered variation on this was observed at a North lawn gathering called "Rural Health Day" held in late May of 1977. Attended by some three hundred mostly Chicano people, when the rally began at about 11:30 a.m. it was announced that the Governor was expected to "come out" and receive their list of demands for state funded health services. If he did not "come out," the rally leader repeated on several occasions, then the crowd would "go in" and "call on" him. By 1:00 p.m. the leader's repetition of this vow was being vigorously received by the crowd and it seemed clear that the throng was prepared noisily to descend en masse on the reception room. That possibility was apparently communicated to the Governor for he appeared a short time later and gave respectful attention to the complex list of requests.

Most quiet and puzzling of the pack-ins were the five occasions in July and August of 1978 in which a medical doctor from a near-by small city led several young couples with children—some thirty people—in protesting inadequate fees paid doctors under the state's health program. Never successful in meeting with officials, they simply sat quietly, sometimes conversing with people waiting to enter the Governor's complex on other business. They also left signed petitions requesting increased fees. One such petition was headed "Medical Fun and Games in the Governor's Office."

The special social and ecological features of the Capitol context embues these pack-ins with "symbolic" features that ought not be allowed to obscure the likely fact that the pack-in in more "intervention" form is probably the most basic and spontaneous unit of social movement unrest and action. In reviewing the historical materials on the unemployed workers' movement of the thirties, for example, Francis Fox Piven and Richard Cloward point up the widespread and frequent descent of demanding crowds on relief offices. In New York alone,

> A survey...revealed that almost all of the forty-two district relief administrators reported frequent dealings with unemployed groups....These groups were disruptive—shouting, picketing, refusing to leave the relief offices...(Piven and Cloward, 1979:67).

Such occurrences were so common that elaborate "rules" for controlling and preventing them were developed, including limiting the size of delegations, frequency of appearance and prohibition of granting demands while "the delegation was on the premises" (Piven and Cloward, 1977:77). Likewise, in the welfare rights movement of the sixties, groups descended on welfare centers demanding that all grievances be settled before the group left, with the threat of a sit-in (Piven and Cloward, 1979:297).

Perhaps attuned to the historical record, social movement strategists and theorists such as Saul Alinsky have even incorporated the pack-in as a standard tool in their repertoire of protest tactics.

Robert Bailey thus reports of one Alinsky-inspired organization in Chicago that visits to the work places of officials often aimed to "disrupt the officials office environment" including such gambits as efforts to "block passageways, pound on doors, and otherwise disrupt standard operations until they receive some form of commitment" (Bailey, 1974:488; see also, Wolfe, 1971).

While similar, the pack-ins at the California Capitol had been tamed and made more media conscious. The microecology of the ground floor of the Capitol and the instant availability of state police constrained "disruption" to noise, crowd motion, and signs. The surface features of disruption were permitted while officials at the same time retained the option of attending or not.

REFERENCES

Assagai, Mel
>1979a ["Governor..."] *Has Terse Meeting With Black Summit Group."* *Sacramento Bee,* June 8.
>1979b *"[Governor...] Promises to Black Summit."* *Sacramento Bee,* August 8.

Bailey, Robert
>1974 *Radicals in Urban Politics: The Alinsky Approach.* Chicago: The University of Chicago Press.

Lofland, John
>1982 *Crowd Lobbying: An Emerging Tactic of Interest Group Struggle.* Davis, CA: Institute for Governmental Affairs.

Magagnini, Stephen
>1979 *"2,000 Here to Chart Black Goals."* *Sacramento Union,* June 6.

McBride, Richard
>1979 *"Unhappy Gas Dealers Meet Here."* *Sacramento Union,* September 1.

Piven, Francis Fox and Richard A. Cloward
>1977 *Poor People's Movements: Why They Succeed, How They Fail.* New York: Vintage Books.

Wolfe, Tom
>1971 *Radical Chic & Mau-Mauing the Flak Catchers.* New York: Bantam.

CHAPTER IV

LONE-INS

The lone protester against injustice is an enshrined element of the Western tradition. Articulated most clearly and forcefully for Americans by Henry David Thoreau (1937) and exemplified in recent times by Rosa Parks on a Montgomery, Alabama bus in 1955 (Piven and Cloward, 1979:208-209), the possibility of doing dramatic solitary witness to a higher morality is familiar to virtually all competent adults and in that sense available as a strategy of ethical and protest action. But even though known, the option is clearly not very often elected. While defined as laudable in some ways, it also smacks of intellectual eccentricity and emotional peculiarity. The potent possibility of so seeming to others is, thus, a powerful deterrent to lone and public protest action.

In the calendar year of 1977, the first author daily monitored the public spaces of the California State Capitol and observed only eleven persons who were not part of a group and were publicly protesting something by carrying a picket sign or handing out handbills. Whether eleven is many or a few depends on one's point of reference, but it strikes us as decidedly few relative to the almost two hundred protesting groups or crowds that were observed over the same period. Vastly larger, also, were the numbers of paid agents of interest groups who trekked daily to the interior portions of the Capitol to promote, protect or enlarge advantages.

Given the media coverage accorded protest occupants of the Governor's reception room, one might expect lone protesters to be disproportionately attracted to that location. Passing out handbills or holding a picket sign alone on a sidewalk is one thing, but occupation of a media floodlighted office is quite another: the latter is vastly more attention attracting and more pointedly directed to officials. But even so, in the six years under consideration, only three lone protesters

39

remained overnight in the reception room at least one night and only three others took up daytime-only vigils.

The initial "lone-inner" also spent the most nights—fourteen between January 12-28, 1976. The action of this champion, a black doctor who practiced in the Watts areas of Los Angeles, was part of a more general turmoil among doctors over skyrocketing costs of medical malpractice insurance. He had been at the Capitol lobbying with other doctors the week previous to his "lone in" and back in Los Angeles he made his decision to occupy the reception room "shortly before dawn" on Monday, January 12th, the first day of his protest occupation (Skelton, 1975). Sitting on his rolled up, orange sleeping bag or on the furniture, he dressed in a white physician's smock and wore a stethoscope around his neck, thus signalling his social role and dignity. Interviewed by reporters, he would explain that although he made $50,000 a year, he was out of work because he could not pay his malpractice insurance premiums. To one reporter he declared "sure it's embarrassing to be sitting here," (Skelton, 1976) but he had to until government found a solution to the problem. Los Angeles Times coverage of his stay printed January 16, 1976 provided a humorous note by picturing the Governor attending the opening of an art exhibit in the reception and adjacent room while the doctor, bedecked in his smock and stethoscope, also sat among the guests. The days wore on and he finally, and simply, left.

The second lone-inner lasted only one night, Monday, January 19th, 1976 and was concurrent with the Los Angeles doctor. The occupier was an elderly woman from San Francisco protesting "curtailment of a federally sponsored and state administered 'escort service'" (Sacramento Bee, 1976). Quoted saying "I'll take one couch and the doctor can have the other," she spoke with a Governor's assistant the next day and then left accompanied by her physician who arrived to express concern about her health.

The third and last sleep-over took place a year and a half later—Thursday night, July 28, 1977—and was performed by a middle-aged woman who was well known for her diverse activism on behalf of the developmentally disabled. A veteran of collective protest occupations directed to Federal and state agencies dealing with such persons (and a leader of the Title XX "spirited seige" described in Chapter VI), she was visiting her teenaged, mentally retarded son at a state hospital near the Capitol the late afternoon of Thursday, July 28, 1977. While there, she became especially agitated over how she found him and other children treated. Among other things, they were dressed for bed just after 6:00 p.m. and locked behind several doors in sweltering heat, she said. On the spot, she decided to take her son, as dressed, to the Governor's reception room and sit there as a protest against conditions in state hospitals. The act was specifically addressed to the Governor for he had toured that same hospital a few days before and, she alleged, had been provided a contrived and specious picture that masked the true and atrocious conditions.

Arriving at the Capitol after 8:00 p.m., she had made it into the building just before it was locked, began calling media, and managed to give a dramatic television interview through the locked (but glass) exterior doors of the Capitol. She slept and sat overnight with her son on the couch in the ground floor women's room. When the Governor's reception room opened in the morning, they took up couch seats in front of the reception desk. On that desk stood a phone that knowledgeable people were aware was available to the use of anyone who asked. Opening the yellow pages to the media listings, she started phoning and by mid-morning assorted print and picture journalists were dutifully interviewing and filming her and her son, the latter of whom squirmed, fidgeted, made a variety of sounds and had almost continually to be restrained. She articulately told her complaints time and time again and called for fundamental reform in the state hospitals, saying that the twenty five or so thousands of dollars spent each year to keep each patient was being wasted. The retarded were merely being warehoused and not trained to care as much as possible for themselves as was the ostensive goal. The Governor seemed more interested in whales and turtles than in people and her presence there was an effort to appeal to the public at large to press for change.

By mid-morning, media coverage had trailed off and she left, returning her son to the hospital.

As mentioned, over the same six years there were also only three people known to have sat in the reception room during ordinary business hours as a form of protest occupation. The earliest, in January, 1976, sat during the day for about a week concurrent with the Los Angeles doctor. He was protesting treatment of people on welfare but spoke to no officials. The second, taking place on Friday, December 2, 1977, was so brief it barely qualifies as a protest occupation. The late afternoon of that day, a lone, middle-aged woman "chained" herself with a bicycle chain and lock to the coffee table located in front of a couch in the Governor's reception office. Her husband was a physician in a nearby small city (the same one leading the groups described in Chapter III, section D) on whose behalf she was expressing her distress that he was losing significant amounts of money treating patients for the fees provided by the state funded health insurance program. A state policeman was assigned to stay with her and in casual conversation between them and with the receptionist, the woman was apprised that late Friday afternoons in December were not attention getting times. She would have to sit there until Monday and the press corps and other people resumed their weekly rounds if she wanted public attention. Expressing disappointment that "no one" was attending and declaring herself tired, she unlocked her chain and left. The episode lasted perhaps two hours.

The last of the day-time-only protesters was a thirty-year old anti-nuclear activist who began a water-only fast at the reception room July 3, 1979. Traveling from his suburban Sacramento home by bicycle and bus, he sat-in daily, calling a press conference on the seventh day of his fast. At it, he vowed to continue until the nearby nuclear generating plant—called Rancho Seco—was closed (Dempster, 1979). He was trying to see the Governor—so far unsuccessfully—in order to ask him to use his emergency powers to shut the plant. He had elected this tactic because "nothing else has worked" (Dempster, 1979), a reference to previous and unsuccessful mass protest, court actions and protest occupations against Rancho Seco. He continued several more days, still did not see the Governor and stopped appearing. However, he returned to the reception room in late 1979 as a core member of the group that staged a thirty-seven night protest occupation with the same objective (an episode recounted in Chapter VII, below).

═══════════

The scarcity and brevity of "lone-ins" suggest, then, a good deal about the need for group—or at least crowd—support in undertaking protest actions even as mildly risky as occupying the Governor's reception room. Moreover, among these few, three were more or less seasoned militants in their respective causes, backgrounds that prepared them for the fearsomeness of "going it alone."

REFERENCES

Dempster, Doug
    1979   "Rancho   Seco   Protester   Enters   Ninth   Day   Fast."
           Sacramento Bee, July 12.
Los Angeles Times
    1976   "Staying Put."   January 16.
Piven, Francis Fox and Richard Cloward
    1979   Poor People's Movements: Why They Succeed, How They
           Fail.   New York: Vintage Books.
Sacramento Bee
    1976   "Another [Governor's name...] Sit-In."   January 21.
Skelton, Nancy
    1976   "LA Doctor Camps in [Governor's] Office in Insurance
           Protest."   Sacramento Bee, January 13.
Thoreau, Henry David
    1937   Walden and Other Writings of Henry David Thoreau.
           New York: Random House.

CHAPTER V

ONE NIGHT STANDS

On six occasions over the six year period, 1975-1980, relatively small groups elected to occupy the reception room only one night in order to make a protest point. These groups were not as "flexed"—meaning loud and raucous—as the pack-ins described above nor as complexly organized as the spirited sieges and vigils to be described in the chapters that follow. They strode, rather, a middle road.

One night stands themselves can be distinguished in terms of having been clearly planned as <u>one</u> night or not. The earliest one appears to have been fielded on the assumption (or at least the public proclamation) that they might go much more than one night, but the response of officials made that unnecessary. Coming one week after a group of farmworkers had initiated protest occupation of the reception room by sleeping over four nights (see Chapter II, section C), a crowd of some sixty mostly wives of medical doctors protesting malpractice insurance costs arrived with sleeping bags, and snacks on December 3, 1975. As upper-middle class women, they seemed, as such, quite a novelty and were even visited by the liberal, black Lieutenant Governor who commented "It's not real, It's too fancy. You're rich. I've been to a lot of picketing in my life..." but, he implied, it never involved their sorts of people (<u>Sacramento Bee</u>, 1975a). The Secretary of Health and Welfare also met with them as did other high officials but the group demanded a meeting with and a commitment to decisive action from the Governor himself. Sleeping-over, they got that meeting the next afternoon and while the Governor did not pledge the special session of the Legislature they desired, he promised to meet with them again at a later time and showed what they took to be genuine concern to achieve remedial action. Having also garnered much media attention, they pronounced their immediate goals attained and left (Fairbanks, 1975a).

It was just one week later that some fifteen parents of retarded children in state hospitals, vowing to stay as long as necessary to see the Governor, slept over one night, Friday, December 12. One of their leaders observed to a Los Angeles Times reporter that they were there because "members of the Legislature and top officials in the state Department of Health...urged us to assume an adversary position because that's what impresses this administration" (Fairbanks, 1975b). Levels of funding in such hospitals was the issue, an issue characterized by the Secretary of Health and Welfare as "very simple. They are asking for $50 million to implement 1973 standards. And I am saying there is not $50 million available" (Sacramento Bee, 1975b).

There were no further one-night stands for almost a year and a half, until late April of 1977, when a group of about twenty five people—four farm worker families—arrived at the reception room seeking the Governor's help in getting permission to live in a migrant labor camp in Monterey County. Having exceeded the 180 day limit on occupancy of such housing, they were at that time "squatting" in make-shift structures just outside the camp they sought to live in. Not able to see the Governor, they stayed overnight in the reception room and the Secretary of Health and Welfare the next day invited them to relocate in his conference room, an invitation they accepted but which had the effect of making them publicly invisible since the Secretary was quartered in the recesses of Office Building Number One, across the street. Shortly, he relocated them in an Army camp (Ramirez, 1977).

Almost a year later, March 13th, 1978, a group of perhaps ten Gray Panthers from San Francisco sought an audience with the Governor in order to get help in forestalling the closure of a nursing home in San Francisco. Their press release declared that the Governor had failed to respond to a February 24 letter requesting an appointment and they had therefore now to appear and "to remain here until we see him and he solves this problem." Their Assemblyperson and a Governor's aide spoke with them but did not act to their satisfaction. Three of them stayed over that night. Still unable to see the Governor, small groups stayed over two other non-adjacent nights later in the month (Sacramento Bee, 1978).

Two, final one-night-stands occurred almost two years later. Both were performed by subgroups of the circle mounting the thirty-seven night vigil of late 1979. The first, involving only four people was a protest comment on reception room seating accommodations initiated the week of February 11th, 1980. The media of Tuesday, February 12th carried pictures of and stories on the previous day's removal of stuffed chairs and couches and their replacement with wooden benches. The stories drew an explicit link between protest and the change of furniture, referring, moreover, to the earlier replacement of carpeting with a hardwood floor (as described in Chapter II, section D). Four of the previous anti-nuclear sit-inners arrived the afternoon of the 12th and stayed one night as a way to say they would not be deterred by such furniture tactics.

Finally, the weekend of March 29-30, 1980 was defined by people in the anti-nuclear movement as the first anniversay of the near-disaster at the Three Mile Island nuclear plant in Middletown, Pennsylvania. Rallies and other protests were put on by the dozens across the country, including one involving about a hundred people held at the headquarters of the municipal utility of Sacramento, the operators of the nuclear power plant called Rancho Seco.

A group of about twenty anti-nuclear protesters who were involved in the previous thirty-seven night occupation (Chapter VII) decided to resume their vigil for the twenty-four hours from noon Friday, March 28 to noon Saturday, March 29. Media flaked, they took up stations on the hard wooden benches and floor. Their numbers declined through the afternoon and six actually slept over under the gaze of a plainclothes state policeman.

They passed their time reading, singing, and chatting with one another. One state policeman assigned to watch them was particularly impressed that at one point they compared how much money they had made the previous year. One was proud to claim, the policeman reported, that he made less than $200 in the last year and another was somewhat embarrassed to admit earning about $8,000. There seemed, in effect, an inverse status hierarchy of income. The core of six consisted of a woman in her fifties who was the leader and five males varying in age from early twenties to mid-thirties. Their grooming and clothes style was ordinary California "collegiate, post-hippy scruffy," referring to faded jeans, head sweat bands, relatively long hair and other such items that are suggestive of identification with underclasses but not true signs of them owing to relatively educated speech and middle-class demeanor.

Shortly past 11:00 a.m. Saturday morning a short man wearing soiled checkered pants, a bright blue windbreaker and a baseball cap inscribed "Golden Bears" arrived at the reception room and broke the silence by embarking on a loud and prolonged stream of verbal abuses of the sit-inners. He swaggered about the room demeaning the Governor, his liberal friends, and all anti-nuclear protesters. The sit-inners tried to respond to his criticism but Golden Bear kept flitting from topic to topic in a decidedly incoherent fashion, making sustained exchange impossible. Soon, in fact, two sit-inners began to ignore his assertions and ask him why he was so angry and unhappy, initiating a therapeutic definition of the situation. The female leader had not been present when Golden Bear arrived and, returning, she assessed the scene and began, with two others, to sing a song. Shortly, all six took it up, one playing a guitar. Golden Bear continued to harangue them, almost oblivious to their chorus, but then fell into silence. He wandered into the main Capitol corridor and plopped down into the elevator operator's chair, staring sullenly away toward the East doors. Through it all, the plainclothes policeman sitting at the receptionist's desk read his newspaper, studiously disattending while attending.

The singing stopped and the sit-inners exchanged remarks on Golden Bear's "borderline psychotic state" and the impossibility of debate with such persons.

A lull ensued. Shortly before noon, they began to pack up their belongings.   Carefully they put their scrap material into the room's wastebasket and, by gesture, obtained the policeman's nodding approval that they were leaving the area in proper order. Just before noon, the leader formed the six into a tight, arms over shoulder circle in which they began to sing, softly and slowly, a mournful song in which the most audible and frequently repeated phrase was "on and on." Accompanied by guitar, the volume and pace of the singing increased until, at the climax, they were shouting in unison at the top of their voices and with revivalistic fervor.   They broke apart at this climax and one of them said, loudly, "let's leave singing."   Continuing to sing spiritedly and at full pitch, they scurried about picking up their coats, books, paper bags, and anti-nuclear placards.   Each nodded grandly to the state policeman who smiled and nodded back.   One smilingly flashed the two finger "V" for peace sign to the policeman.   The last person to exit the room, the female leader, stopped in the corridor just outside the room, faced into the room and performed a deep formal bow as though giving homage—perhaps mock homage—to the shrine of state power, the Governor's reception room.   Still singing, they exited the East doors.

As though it was utter routine—as it indeed was—the policeman immediately closed and locked the two large doors to the reception room and went about other duties.

―――――――――

We may think of pack-ins, lone-ins, and one-night-stands as forming a class of relatively "short burst" protest action. A "strong" but brief public expression is mounted and one settles, at the time, for whatever can be achieved in that burst.   It may be that one even predetermines to settle for having only made a public declaration of sentiment.   Such an aim is seen clearly in the two anti-nuclear sit-ins just described where the groups appear beforehand to have decided l) to stay only one night and 2) not to attempt directly to influence the Governor or other local officials.   They, that is, were sitting-in for the public and declarative effect of their actions, a goal achieved by garnering media coverage. The goal and achievement was in this way rather like the goal and achievement of Memorial Day and Fourth of July observances: one calls attention to a general class of sentiments rather than negotiates specific social changes.   Such a goal and achievement is seen, likewise, in many of the pack-ins and lone-ins reviewed in the two preceding chapters.

Of course, some members of episodes among these three micro forms of protest occupation were more than happy to negotiate specifically and pointedly with officials and a few even seem to have felt they had, at the time, made significant progress, as, for example, the doctors' wives. None, however, seem fully to have gotten what they specifically wanted "on the spot," given that their desires often involved large sums of money, multi-stepped and therefore temporarily prolonged change procedures, and multiple centers of power (namely, the Legislature). The Governor and his administration, that is, might display much sympathy and support and still not fulfill demands because they did not have the power <u>immediately</u> to do so. Hence, short burst protest could at best extract pledges of "looking into" and "considering" demands.

A handful of episodes, though, wanted more and strove to construct "longer burst" protest that achieved real action at the time. It is to these that we now turn in the form of spirited sieges and long-term vigils.

REFERENCES

Fairbanks, Robert
    1975a "Sleep-Over: Public's Eyes Opened?"   Los Angeles Times, December 5.
    1975b "[Governor's]...Office Invaded by Third Sit-in in 3 Weeks." Los Angeles Times, December 13.
Ramirez, Raul
    1977 "Migrants win housing battles."   San Francisco Sunday Examiner and Chronicle, May 1.
Sacramento Bee
    1975a "Malpractice Sleep-In in...[Governor's] Office." December 4.
    1975b "Retarded-Child Parents Stage...[Governor's] Office Sit-in." December 13.
    1978 "Gray Panthers Occupy Governor's Office."   March 22.

CHAPTER VI

SPIRITED SIEGES

As indicated in Chapter II, the array of protest occupations we are considering differed markedly in overall level of "flex" or mobilization by which is meant the frequency, duration and level of collective singing, chanting, parading, marching and other noisemaking and crowd locomotion. The pack-ins reported in Chapter III displayed a relatively high level of such flex, albeit pack-in episodes were brief and thereby so limited. Lone-ins and one-night stands tended, overall, to relatively low levels of flex, even though there might be high moments, as in the exiting flex of the Three Mile Island memorial sit-in described at the end of the last chapter.

We come now to two protest occupations that exhibited the highest levels of flex observed at the Capitol. The judgment of "highest" does not at all mean that the crowds involved sang and so forth anywhere near "all the time." Instead, they flexed with regularity and as a conspicuous feature of their strategy of protest occupation. In shear clock time, high flex was a small portion of their total time on the premises, but even so, high flex was exhibited at times and places that were obtrusive and dramatic, thus imbuing the total effort with an ambience of high, collective arousal.

A high level of flex appears to combine with a mid-length of protest occupation. That is, the two rather intense episodes described below lasted, respectively, two nights and three days and three nights and four days. Pack-ins, in contrast, took their best shot, so to speak, and left, knowing beforehand they would be leaving in a short time. Lone-ins and one-night stands made a slightly longer and lower key burst and left. The two "spirited sieges" seen now conjoined the high flex of the pack-in with the greater persistence of the one-night stand.

A. THE DEAF/BLIND COALITION

The night of Tuesday, June 21st and into the dark morning hours of Wednesday, June 22nd, 1977, a chartered bus stopped at several preplanned locations in the Los Angeles area, picking up clusters of blind and deaf people. Traveling North some 400 miles, late morning the 22nd the group arrived at the office of the State Director of Rehabilitation in Office Building Number One, across the street from the Capitol, to complain that an organizationally independent but state funded program called the Client Assistance Program (CAP) was being discontinued June 30th and replaced by an in-house ombudsman scheme more under the control of that Director. Despite several hours of spirited talk, the Director would not relent in the discontinuance and replacement.

The leaders thereupon redirected their appeal to the Director's superior, the Secretary of Health and Welfare, and strategized to get his immediate attention by proceeding to the Governor's reception room and sitting-in. Media were phoned and coverage began Wednesday afternoon, coverage that featured the terms "blind" and "disabled" linked to the word "protest." Some of the more disabled returned to Los Angeles on Wednesday, but about thirty vowed to stay until CAP was "saved," the concrete instrument of its salvation being Senate Bill 1138.

The protesters themselves were almost all teachers of the blind or deaf, deaf or blind college students, and professionals or aides employed by organizations serving these two kinds of disablements. That is, the small crowd was educated and articulate. The three prime leaders of the sit-in were the heads of their respective organizations, organizations that advocated on behalf of their particular disabilities. The "leader of the leaders," as he emerged, was a blind teacher in his thirties who dressed in neatly pressed polyester leisure suits. We may refer to him here as Bill.

The Secretary himself appeared at the reception room and spoke with the group several hours Wednesday evening. The Governor's Chief of Staff, a staff aide for employee relations, and another aide also participated in the meeting. At loggerheads, they all decided to meet again at 9:00 a.m. Thursday.

As in other sit-ins, only token members actually slept over the entire night during this sit-in. The first night, Wednesday, this was a handful of mostly young students. The leaders and others stayed in a hotel about a block away.

The next morning, a delegation of half a dozen was led by aides to the Health and Welfare Secretary's office. Returning at midmorning, the Secretary was reported unchanged, but he had promised to meet with them yet again in the reception room at 3:30 p.m. that day. This announcement was greeted with crowd chanting of "We want [The Secretary]" and singing of a morale song used by one of the organizations for the blind and set to the tune of the "Battle Hymn of the Republic." The support of the Chicano and Black caucuses of the Legislature was announced and greeted with loud cheering and clapping.

Also this morning, the sighted aides had written up, duplicated and distributed a press release to the nearby offices of the capitol press corps. The late morning and early afternoon was an orgy of media cameras and their associated floodlights. Blind and deaf people, it could be surmised, made unusual media pictures and sound. A large portion of the blind, for example, carried distinctive long canes and had closed eyelids. Some of the deaf spoke in an unusual manner or made hand signs. In addition, several small placards proclaiming the cause were hand-held or leaned against chairs and tables. Expressions included "Don't Cop Out, Keep CAP" and "Put CAP back into handicap." Perhaps most photographed was the German Shepard seeing-eye dog that belonged to one of the young, female sit-inners.

At the late morning height of this media orgy about a dozen mostly Asian American people arrived at the reception room to meet with Governor's aides in order to "protest" a certain physician's nomination to the State Board of Medical Quality Assurance. Liberally distributing their press release letterheaded Chinese for Affirmative Action (CAA), media turned to interviewing them and there ensued a degree of confusion as to who was protesting what in what manner. The CAA spokesperson commented that there "looks like some competition in terms of the room space for a full-fledged sit-in," thus intimating that their sit-in had been aborted for want of a site. The group met with Governor's aides and left.

Because of blindness, the largest portion of these sit-inners were cumbersomely mobile and therefore less able to disband and reassemble in a more private place for strategy and morale building sessions. Instead, their strategy and morale building meetings were held in the reception room, "before the public," as it were. Sporadically, Bill, the leader of the leaders, announced or at least exhorted plans and actions and admonished persistence as in: "You guys don't know how great it is to have you here because that is our strength because they want us out of here." The coalition between the deaf and blind was extolled with such phrases as "our brothers."

By mid-day Thursday, Bill and others were directing that people should, in relays, visit the offices of legislators in support of SB 1138, a relay activity that went on Thursday afternoon and Friday.

Late June was a peak tourist group visiting time at the Capitol and through Thursday and Friday various adult and children's groups paused by the open reception room doors, curiously eyeing all the people with long canes and closed eyes. One tour guide even incorporated the sit-inners into her running spiel, referring to them as "people waiting to see the Governor." These clusters of starers were all the more noticeable because many of them were uniformed, as in Boys' State T-shirts, Cub Scout outfits and Christian choir suits and long dresses.

The reception room scene these touring children and adults beheld was all the more curious because of its unusual barrenness. The walls of the room ordinarily featured "art" or other displays that communicated the interests or at least the blessings of the Governor's administration. In 1977, for example, the walls were used for exhibits on whales, space, and the art of (ironically) retarded adults and people in state prisons. The deaf-blind sit-in occurred between exhibits and the faded and dirty wall covering of the reception room was especially noticeable. The large glass display case in the room was also empty and combined with the sundry suitcases, sleeping bags and cardboard boxes of the sit-inners, the scene was reminiscent of a seedy bus stop waiting room.

From time to time on Thursday and Friday, members of the Legislature stopped by and addressed the lounging group, pledging support of their cause, SB 1138. They also urged the sit-inners to persist.

The Secretary did not appear at 3:30 p.m. on Thursday as he had promised. The tens of minutes went by after the appointed time and Bill gave pep talks, emphasizing that they were "getting media twenty-four hours a day." He stressed that "we have to have strength," acknowledging the particular difficulties of the diabetics in the group. The theme song of one of their organizations was sung, "Glory, Glory Federation" (to the tune of the Battle Hymn of the Republic) and there were chantings of "We Want [the Secretary's first name]." The singing and chanting grew sporadic and toward 5:30 p.m. there was an element of giddiness in the group atmosphere signaled by a good deal of giggling and joking.

The Secretary finally appeared at 6:30 p.m., apologizing for his lateness, and announced he did not want to decide on SB 1138 at that moment. He would prefer to sit down and talk about it another time. The group insisted on an answer there and then. In that case, he said, his answer was no. He supported the end of CAP and the start of the Director's in-house program. The Secretary thereupon left the reception room and chants of "We Want [the Governor]" went up. In the discussion that followed, Bill and others accused the Secretary of "bad faith." They must now "wait until the public comes in tomorrow and build further pressure, shifting their appeal, now, to the Governor.

An interlude of watching/listening television coverage of them (on a member's small set) followed. When found by switching among newscasts, it provoked cheers. A senator stopped by and urged them to "stay with it" for "they were doing the right thing." An aide to the Secretary arrived to report that the Secretary was ready to meet with them again, the next day, at noon. Heartened, a strategy talk ensued, stressing that the Secretary had "broke his faith with us" especially in arriving three hours late for his appointment. By about 7:00 p.m., Bill's declaration that they should stay in the reception room this second night was greeted with cheers. Various people drifted out and the quiet of evening settled in beneath the eye of the plainclothes state policeman who sat at the reception desk.

Mid-evening, what appeared to be a young and cub reporter arrived at the reception room, saying to Bill "I'm new on this, what is the issue here?" Bill expended an exhausted breath and drew himself up to launch, for the several dozenth time that day, into the story, starting from the beginning.

Friday morning in the reception room was much quieter than Thursday—many fewer media people appeared—and the group's effort went into gathering ever-more legislative support for SB 1138.

The director of the threatened CAP program (who was a "temporarily abled bodied person," as one sometimes heard it put) had himself been present in most of the scenes described above and there was a certain tension between him and the disabled leaders over who could speak for them all. (They existed in the ironic relation of the disabled trying to save his job so he could advocate for them in bureaucratic matters but yet they were carrying the advocacy burden in this sit-in effort.) Late Thursday morning, this director got into a chance hallway conversation just outside the reception room with a hot-headed Governor's aide who had been present but had not spoken in a previous meeting with the disabled. One exchange led to another and, shortly, the CAP director and he were in a hallway shouting match that quickly collected a crowd and several media teams. Embarrassed to have become a Capitol hallway sideshow, the two of them broke it off within a few minutes but that show of aggression served to discredit the CAP director in subsequent decision-making and he was infrequently present from that point to the end of the sit-in. The episode evoked among the blind and disabled numerous expressions of a strong preference for coolness as a petitioning style along with frequent additional expressions of the necessity for the disabled to speak for themselves.

In the late morning it was announced that 76 of 80 Assemblypersons and 30 of 40 Senators had signed a letter supporting SB 1138, a feat credited heavily to the efforts of an aide to the Senator carrying SB 1138.

At mid-day, the leadership circle met with the Health and Welfare Secretary again, in his office, and returned to report a modified stance. The Secretary had promised them an important advising role in the new ombudsman program. Nothing was written but these leaders believed they would themselves be appointed to the formal, advisory commission that was now to be a feature of the program, or at least they would have a critical voice in who was appointed. Said to be equally as important, the Secretary had promised to deal with them directly in the future, and not through the director of rehabilitation. This, said Bill, was an important step, for they now "dealt at a higher level." Moreover, he also promised no reprisals over this episode of protest.

However, they still had to support SB 1138 but even if they lost on it, they had a victory. Several of the college student participants expressed their disappointment with these announcements. Exchanges ensued and the session trailed off indecisively. Relative silence settled on the reception room in the early afternoon. People continued to go into the upper floors of the Capitol in order to lobby. Bits of "gallows humor" were heard among those sitting about the reception room:

[Commenter, to group:]	Let's got to the library and get a book on "how to get to the Governor."
[Group laughter]	
[Another commenter:]	We're becoming experts on how not to get in!

In the afternoon little was spoken about it but the critical question facing them was whether to sleep over that night, a question that was all the more critical since this was Friday and there was little or no possibility of further, political action before Monday. In addition, they had heard that the Govenor had left the city for the weekend. A meeting with him was impossible before Monday. Sporadically in the afternoon, news of more support came and Bill exhorted the group to "Keep the Faith." A new memo of support signed by several legislators and containing sixty-five dollars in cash arrived and was greeted with cheers.

But the unspoken problem they faced continued: to leave or to stay? As seems to be the case with all crowds, the size of this one had been dwindling from the start and they were now down to about a dozen; that, too, had to be considered. It seemed also that the prospect of a dreary weekend in that room was uninviting to all. But the question was, how to leave with grace?

At the noon meeting, the Secretary had told the leaders he might stop by and see them again late in this day and he, indeed, appeared shortly before 6:00 p.m. Bill called the group into quiet attention and introduced the Secretary in these spirited words: "Ladies and Gentlemen, we are very proud to have here—he said he would try to come by—the Secretary of the Health and Welfare Agency [his full name is given]." Mild applause greeted the introduction and the Secretary made brief, low-keyed remarks on how decisions are "difficult and agonizing" and that while he supported the department's plan over SB 1138, they had his

> personal pledge I will do all I can to insure
> the ombudsman program is fully implemented
> and becomes workable.   [Futher,] I'll be
> available [and] I'll meet...personally [with
> those involved].

He was loudly applauded on finishing, chatted with leaders for a few minutes, and left. With that, Bill announced his assessment that they had achieved a great deal in the past three days and that they could now leave. He elaborated their accomplishments as being strong legislative support for SB 1138, which they might still get enacted, and the opening of channels to higher levels than ever before. Previously, they had not been able to meet with the Secretary or the Governor's Chief of Staff, acts they had now performed and could continue to do. Waxing rhetorical, he declared: "The blind and the deaf are now taken more seriously....This is power politics. We had important people sit down and deal with us. We are changing the image of the blind and the deaf." Moreover, said Bill, the Governor left town in order to avoid dealing with them. People began gathering up their belongings and Bill loudly commended everyone several times: "I thank you and I think you are all beautiful." Scattering in cliques, the sit-in was over shortly before 7:00 p.m.

Attention should be called to the fact that this seemed a definitely "non-threatening" affair to officials, especially the State Police. The observer-author was particularly struck by the on-duty plainclothes policeman and receptionist's "here-we-go-again" smiles to each other when the crowd cheered the group decision that they would sleep over in the reception room on Thursday night. As reported, the group had abundant and important legislative visitors and supporters. Police were only minimally present and in plainclothes. Such a "low profile" was, of course, not unrelated to the fact that many of the sit-inners were blind and deaf. Their most visible leader was, moreover, short, chubby, and spoke in a high voice.

One interesting generalization suggested about this attention getting tactic is that when played out within the rules, the merely normal cycles of public attending can leave the actors impaled on their own technique. Of what use is an attention getting act such as sitting-in that no one attends to? The problem is then that of getting out of it gracefully. In this episode, the Secretary's last and solicitous appearance provided a vehicle for such an "out." Had he not appeared, departure would doubtless have been even more painful.

B. THE TITLE XX COALITION

A rather pure state of flux would presumably consist of an unrelenting, large crowd moving about and making noise without pause and thereby disrupting local routines. The finitude of protester energy and resources and the definite limits of authority's forebearance render this, of course, a mere theoretical possibility. However, while far from a pure case, the protest occupation of the Title XX coalition moved clearly in that direction over its four-day life from the late morning of Monday, June 27 through the early morning hours of Friday, July 1, 1977.

The matter at issue is key to understanding the flex level and pattern of the sit-in; that is, there was an unusual dove-tailing of the demand being made and the social organization of the protest. The state budget passed by the Legislature and sent to the Governor the weekend previous to the Title XX sit-in provided 18.9 million dollars in "augmentation" to make up for Federal withdrawal from paying for community centers for the developmentally handicapped." People involved in such centers were concerned that the Governor might strike the augmentation. Effects of that would be felt immediately on July 1. At least some of the staff involved in the sit-in might be out of work by the end of the week, many believed, and a range of center-sponsored services which involved recreation and job training would be cut. The system of centers was itself a part of the state strategy to "deinstitutionalize" as many of the developmentally handicapped as possible, but cuts would mean that many center clients would be sent back to state hospitals.

Because of the particular transportation problems of the developmentally disabled in the community, many centers had purchased specially outfitted vans and a few localities, nearby San Francisco in particular, had elaborated virtual fleets of them that constituted, functionally, an alternate transport system. In addition to carrying clients to and from centers, these vehicles were often used for camping and picnic excursions, a mode of transport that made the handicapped less obtrusive in the community.

The protest mobilization potential of all this is obvious. Hundreds of the Northern California handicapped who were daily delivered to centers in order to recreate and do other things and were sometimes taken on day trips could almost as easily be taken to the Capitol. Phrased differently, there was here: a) routine congregation of people, b) with free time, c) possessing transportation, d) deployable social organization and skilled leaders, and e) other routine support facilities such as a regular flow of food. With regard to social organization, the participants were clearly stratified into three highly auspicious categories: 1) middle-aged and slightly younger administrators and free-floating activists at the top who were the leaders (an officer class); hired, young adults who were the on-line caretakers of the retarded (non-commissioned officer class); and 3) the developmentally disabled themselves who were the malleable troops of the sit-in.   The leaders plotted the action, the staff herded and cajoled the troops and the troops more or less did what they were told.   We say "more or less" because it was difficult to hold their attention.   On the other hand, they presented no problem of ideological or tactical dissent, problems that did appear among leaders and between leaders and staff.

The numbers of people in each category present on the scene expanded and contracted through the several flex and repose phases. Overall, leaders varied from about five to fifteen; staff varied from about fifteen to fifty and troops varied from about 15 to 350.

Beginning to converge on the Capitol North Lawn late Monday morning, June 27, the crowd numbered about three-hundred during the lunch hour and early afternoon.   While eating lunch several of the "recreation leaders," as staff were sometimes also labeled, set up a large loudspeaker system and conducted a rally, urging the crowd to sing along with such songs as "This Land Is My Land," an effort only partially successful since a large portion of the crowd seemed to have some difficulty singing.   Several of the retarded were called forth to give short pep talks on the necessity to keep the centers open.   While staff thusly occupied the troops, the leaders, numbering about a dozen, huddled beneath a nearby tree divising strategy, strategy that included the explicitly articulated principle of leaving one's plans open for emergent possibilities and not locking into any fixed, long-term notions.   At this time, that principle meant they had not yet decided if they would sit-in.

Shortly past 1:00 p.m., the crowd was led singing and clapping into the ground floor Capitol corridor.   One segment of it entered and milled about the Governor's reception room led by a guitar playing staffer who shouted to the troops: "We want to sing to [The Governor's Chief of Staff].   You can tell them that we want our services, so that is why you are going to keep on singing.   If [the Chief] isn't there we are going to find his office."   A loud cheer went up and singing ensued.   A second and the largest segment more or less walked in an oval in the main Capitol hallway and sang.   A third segment washed into the outer offices of the State Director of Finance, a complex immediately inside the Capitol north doors.   This segment chanted, to a leader, "Please Mr..... [Finance Director] don't send us back to Hell."   (The word "hell" rhymed with the Director's last name.)   The Finance Director allowed ten or so of them into his office along with a uniformed State Policeman and a reporter who was conspicuously recording the encounter.   The leaders' talk stressed the year-in, year-out indeterminacy of their funding and the cruelty of not yet having made a decision on the fate of the centers.   On his side, the Director pleaded that he would follow the advice of the Health and Welfare Department: "I told you people the Health Department is [sic] the experts and we expect them to tell us what is right."   Having thus removed himself from the line of decision, the group's energy was somewhat blocked but then redirected when the Director also told them that he had been told that the Governor's Chief of Staff would meet with them shortly.   The troops of retarded were directed out of the Finance offices and into the already crowded Governor's reception room.   There, they waited and sang several songs including the sixties classic, "Blowing in the   Wind."

Close to 2:00 p.m. the Chief appeared, flanked by a plainclothes policeman and a Governor's staff person.   The crowd quieted and one of the leaders addressed the Chief, loudly for all to hear, including several reporters who had been attracted by all the crowd commotion. They had three questions, the leader said: 1) the status of the 18.9 million, 2) the source of those funds, and 3) possibilities for forming an on-going policy so that they would not have to come back in this fashion every year.   The Chief dealt cautiously with each.   There would be some funding, but the amount was not yet clear.   They had to talk to the Secretary of Health and Welfare about "the needs" and to consider all of them, a suggestion that met with boos and other sounds of crowd displeasure.   The money, he continued, would come from the general fund of the state.

Several exchanges ensued and the talk became increasingly heated in tone and multi-nucleated in character.   The scene was shortly one of "hub bub" in which the Chief would address a given person but could not be heard above people trying simultaneously to address him and/or muttering among themselves.

An angry parent who was shouting louder than other people presently gained the floor and berated the Chief because the Governor had broken his campaign promises to the handicapped.   Her denunciations were met with fervent supportive applause.   The Chief responded by quoting statistics to the effect that there had been large increases already.   Quieting the crowd, another leader asked the Chief if the Health and Welfare Secretary supported the 18.9 million request would the Governor go along?   He replied that in that event, they would be "ninety percent home" and added that he had talked to the Health and Welfare Secretary that day who had said he could meet with these citizens at 3:30 p.m. or so this afternoon.

As did the Finance Director, the Chief of Staff had now turned them to yet another person, a turn members of the crowd did not accept calmly.   Exchanges between them and the Chief continued and encompassed an expanding array of discontents.   One young staffer stressed that it was all "a tremendously frustrating experience to [have] to come up here."   A parent complained about low earning limitations and associated loss of services, a point that rapidly escalated into insults that were themselves called to a halt by one of the leaders who ordered that everyone go back outside for a break before meeting with the Health and Welfare Secretary.

Outside, under the huge shade tree on the North Capitol lawn, a major constraint of the retarded as protesters began to appear: They were due to return to their homes by evening. Protest or not, most of them had to be started back to San Francisco in the mid-afternoon. The convoy of specially equipped vans were brought close to the North lawn and loading began. About half of the high point three hundred were gone by 3:00 p.m., prompting a staffer worriedly to observe, "We are losing people fast."

The Health and Welfare Secretary arrived close to 3:30 p.m., met with the leaders in the conference room behind the Governor's reception room, made no promises, and left. A few minutes after 4:00 p.m. the leaders made the decision to sit-in. Referred to among them as putting "plan A into effect," it was a contingency for which they had made detailed preparations. The sit-inners were a small, elite corps of previously selected, most reliable and least problematic retarded who were cared for by a one-to-one ratio of staff, staff who had volunteered for this sit-in duty. Totaling about thirty, virtually all came from a certain center for the retarded in San Francisco.

The decision having been made, sleeping bags, blankets, ice chests, suitcases and assorted other items were brought by staff from the vans into the reception room. That is, they had come well prepared.

From the period of relative flex, the episode went into a night of repose under the ever-on fluorescent ceiling lights of the reception room and the hourly change of the watch of plainclothes state policemen.

The guidelines of the sit-in were negotiated with the State Police at about 6:30 p.m. A State Police Commander announced that the main rule was that no one could go in or out of the building or be in the hallway after 9:00 p.m. (thus cutting off access to the toilets). No mattresses and no phone calls. One of the more activist of the leaders, a young, white male in a wheel chair and veteran of disableds' sit-ins at Federal offices in Washington and San Francisco, took such rules to be merely "their gound rules." Countering that other people's luxuries were the disabled's necessities, he got most of the rules dropped or relaxed. In so pushing and gaining concessions, this person was explicitly aware that, as he put it, "we get away with things we never could if we weren't handicapped."

Even though the corps of people preselected to sleep over in the reception room totaled about thirty, only eighteen of them—nine staff, nine disabled—were so deployed the first night. All the leaders either went home and returned the next day or slept elsewhere in the city.

Utilizing the facilities of supportive political figures and local organizations for the retarded, a press release was written and circulated to press corp offices early Tuesday morning. It appeared to have contributed to producing a reasonable press turn out at the reception room press conference the leaders held at mid-morning. About one hundred retarded and other staff had also arrived by the time of the press conference. They milled in the reception room and hall. Late in the morning, a token force was left in the reception room and the main body ascended to the large open-air patio on the third floor of the Capitol building. There, with the disabled paying little attention, the leaders and staff held an assessment, strategy, and pep talk meeting. Among the items: a local charity would be providing some free meals; requests for meetings with several high officials had been made but not yet confirmed; officials were "running scared to a degree;" strength had to be marshalled this day, but the large push would be on Wednesday. One of the staff members complained to the assembly that, to him, their effort lacked sufficient organization and arrangements for letting people know "what is going on." The leaders responded with the proposal to create a set of committees, including a "steering committee." The members of the committees, especially the steering one, would be representatives chosen by the organizations participating in the coalition. After more discussion, the dozen people who defined themselves as representing a participating organization huddled in one corner of the patio and soon emerged with an eleven person steering committee and eight other committees. The list codified the existing three-tiered stratification system. That is, no retarded persons were on the list and only a few staff people occupied policy positions. Further, the personal basis of power was revealed in that the single person who controlled the most resources—the staff bodies, vans, the sleeping-over retarded—but who was also not especially assertive served only on the "food and clean up" and "PR" committees. Two other people, each of whom claimed to represent an organization although they were the sole member of each present at the sit-in, were on all the key committees and virtually ran the sit-in. One was the young, wheelchaired male mentioned above and the other was a middle-aged woman we may refer to as Citizen's Advocate. A month later she would sit over one night in the reception room with her retarded son, an episode that has been described in Chapter IV. Like the wheelchaired male, she was a veteran of several sit-ins for the retarded, including the historic ones in Washington and San Francisco in 1976 and 1977.

The meeting concluded with the Wheelchair Activist urging that they revisit the Finance Director to see if he now possessed the information he had yesterday said he was waiting to receive before he could answer all their questions. Further, said Wheelchair Activist, "If he is not there, I suggest we all stay there." This proposed action was accepted without discussion or debate and set, further, in this context by him:

> We are here to make it difficult for them to
> work because they refused to meet our needs.

We are [not, therefore] going to make it easy
for them to meet their needs.

*   *   *

[Morever, as a matter of strategy:]   There
ought to be something happening all the time.

A noon-time lull followed while staff fed the retarded from stores
brought with them from their respective cities of origin, mostly
San Francisco.

Shortly after 1:00 p.m. the slowly increasing crowd of day-trippers
was approaching 200, a good portion of which began crowding sardine-like
into the outer offices of the Finance Director, led by a guitar strumming
staffer in singing "We Shall Overcome," "Amen," and other songs. Chants
interspersed the singing, including "We Want [First and last name of the
Finance Director] repeated faster and faster and faster to a climax. A
uniformed State Police person arrived and told them to keep a path
through the office clear and then he stood by, watching the scene. There
were other chants and songs as the temperature of the room rose due
to the heat given off from so many close and active bodies. The woman
we are calling Citizen Advocate seemed in charge of this action and
about 1:30 p.m. she raised her hand for the crowd to be quiet. The din
subsided and she announced that the Director did not seem to be in his
office. Did they want to wait or leave? Shouts of "wait" went up and
a new lower-key period of quieter singing and chanting ensued. Citizen
Advocate again called for quiet and announced that they might speak
with a Director's aide who is there. A chant calling for the aide arose
but she declined to appear before the packed crowd.

Again there was a lull. The heat from the almost 200 wall-to-wall
retarded packed into the narrow room of desks was becoming intense.
Individuals began to drift out and stand about in the main Capitol hall
or to go outside on the North Capitol lawn. By 2:30 p.m. most of the
retarded had left the office area and at that point the remaining waiters
were simply filed out.

Pursuing the idea of "something happening all the time," Wheelchair
Activist promptly enlisted the leaders and staff in a plan to occupy a
conference room in the Controller's office complex, also on the ground
floor of the Capitol. Wary of State Police, two uniformed members of
which were lounging watchfully in the groundfloor hall, the participants,
including about a hundred day-tripping disabled, were packed into the
reception room. At 3:35 p.m., the largest portion of this crowd was
started out of the reception room and down the main Capitol hall to
the West, as though once more moving on the offices of the Finance
Director. The two state policemen began to move along with them. A

"shock troop" squad of about fifteen, mostly staff and led by the rangy and fast moving Wheelchair Activist, then darted out of the reception room under the cover of the crowd and to the East, bursting through the closed doors of the Controller's office. Previously unknown to them, a state police office happened also to be in the Controller's complex and several high ranking members of the force immediately appeared, ordered them out of the complex, and without fanfare or discussion bodily removed the more physically disabled and simply wheeled out the Wheelchair Activist. The episode was over in but a few minutes and was followed by six uniformed police now being stationed in the main Capitol halls.

Back in the reception room, the Health and Welfare Secretary appeared, unannounced, at 4:00 p.m. Present for about ten minutes, he reported himself not yet prepared to give them "a figure." He listed several reports he had to study and meetings he had yet to attend before he could decide. He would have an answer by Thursday, though. The crowd, now back in the reception room, moaned its displeasure; someone shouted the word "disgusting." Citizen Advocate accused him of perversely enjoying this torturing exercise of power, this game of "playing cat and mouse." Generalized hub-bub arose and shortly before leaving, the Secreatry agreed to have lunch with them on Wednesday, saying, with seemingly humorous intent, "I want three tacos," a remark that only he found funny. As he left, the staff-led crowd began singing "We Are Overcome."

With this, the flex part of the day ended. An element of the elite corps of staff and disabled slept over that Tuesday night which was uneventful save for two retarded women who became enraged with one another and fought briefly, parted by police and staff.

Wednesday morning was also uneventful in anticipation of the larger noon-time action with the Secretary. However, the State Police indicated that morning that there were to be no television sets, coffee pots or food in the reception room, an order a response to which the leaders were delaying until the afternoon.

The crowd of retarded began arriving in the late morning and numbered perhaps 200 by noon, building to over 300 in the early afternoon, arriving sporadically from centers in several Northern California cities.

Lunch with the Secretary was to be on the Capitol West lawn rather than on the more publicly visible North lawn. (This shift was necessary because several hundred nursing home employees had sometime previously reserved the North lawn for their picketing activity.) The gradually assembling crowd was "warmed up" by staff leading peppy songs including "Josuah Fit the Battle of Jericho" refitted with such lyrics as "Governor [name] Sign the Bill." Leaders informed the crowd that the Secretary would not be allowed to address them unless he promised to endorse the entire 18.9 million dollars. And if he so endorsed, any cheering was for themselves, not for the Secretary. Further, if he did not give support, there was a new song to sing to him, a song the leaders, as a chorus, then taught to their charges. Taking off from the Secretary's alleged habit of putting his arm around people, the key line went "If he pats you on the shoulder, turn away." A second hostile song was also taught, the refrain of which went "For [the Secretary] is a blotta, cause he won't do what he otta." (The Secretary's last name somewhat rhymed with "blotta" and "otta.") So prepared, the lunch-munching crowd waited and sang. As 1:00 p.m. approached and the Secretary had still not appeared, the leaders concluded they had been "stood up" and so advised their people:

> [He] broke our date because he had to go see the other group that is demonstrating because apparently they are more important than we are. What does that say to you? [Loud crowd boos.]

*   *   *

> The game is playing the groups against each other.

Leaders declared they knew the Secretary was in the Capitol building and they needed therefore to go inside and march and sing in the ground floor halls until he came out. And that they did. Swelled to their maximum numbers of over 300, for that day, at just past 1:00 p.m., the troops were formed into a single column that marched in a long "L" shape that fitted the ground floor Capitol hallways. The singing and chanting sounds bounced off the bare marble and glass surfaces creating an enormous din. Hurriedly, leaders strove to find media people to film this new, dramatic and interior performance, but few responded. After some twenty-five minutes, the troops were ordered to sit down along the corridor walls and rest. A few minutes later they were gotten back up to march, sing and chant again. This mini-cycle of flex and relax repeated several times. By about 2:30 p.m. the day-trippers were leaving in a steady flow and almost half had already gone. By 3:15, only about 50 were left and the marching, chanting and singing were stopped.

Having met with no official concerning the 18.9 million that day, the sit-in again settled back into a state of repose with its leaders now strategizing the character of the flex for the next day, Thursday, the last day of the month and the day by the end of which they would know the fate of the appropriation.

Late this afternoon, Wheelchair Activist answered the State Police order, mentioned above, to remove various items from the reception room. In a hallway encounter among the Capitol Commander, several leaders, and some staff, Wheelchair Activist argued that removing their equipment from the building was a special hardship owing to the disabilities of many of the participants. After much back and forth and repetitive talk where each repeated his understanding to the other, it was agreed that they only had to take their equipment out of the reception room rather than the building. Concretely, this meant stacking it along the walls of the main floor corridors, which they did. The Commander thus got the reception room a bit cleared, at the expense of a cluttered hallway, and the sit-inners got to keep their equipment close by.

Some forty people slept-over Wednesday night, a part of them using the office areas of two friendly Legislators whose offices were on the upper floors of the Capitol building.

A Thursday morning meeting had been scheduled with the Secretary but he called and canceled at the last minute. No other contact with officials was scheduled for the day. That morning, the four main leaders appeared rather haggard and subdued. Wheelchair Activist had left the premises late Wednesday, claiming the press of business in the Los Angeles organization for the handicapped he headed. His absence as the assertive sparkplug was noticeable. Further, a competing social event in San Francisco, the source of a large portion of the midday trippers, would reduce the size of the crowd available for this afternoon "flex," a reduction leaders planned to compensate for by making more noise.

The arriving troops numbered perhaps two hundred just past noon when they assembled to rally on the North lawn. For about forty-five minutes, there was singing punctuated by pep talks from several of the retarded. The pep talks included such loudly applauded promulgations as:

The Governor is crazy if he does not sign

*   *   *

...break that damn, fucking door.

*   *   *

[Governor's nick name and last name] is crazy; he is stupid.

*   *   *

Going to beat his butt if he doesn't sign.

*   *   *

I don't think he has the right to close down anything.

Members of the audience acted in a manner reminiscent of revivals, yelling out "right on," "yeah, yeah," and other terms of agreement.

Just past 1:00 p.m., the crowd was moved into the Capitol ground floor and marched about as was done the previous day. This day, though, was different than the day before in four principal respects. One, more instruments accompanied the singing, including, most noticeably, a wastebasket the bottom of which was used as a drum. The collective noise was almost deafening. Two, the singing and chanting were more intense, rhythmic or even "primitive" as such things are conveyed in the imagries provided by Hollywood movies that show dances in "primitive societies." The rhythmical songs included "Josuah Fit the Battle" done to the words "Hey, Governor [name] please sign the bill." Chants included "If you think it's loud it's gonna get louder, sign the bill now" and "We want [Governor's nick name and last name]." Three, marching in a ring through the halls and the collective noise went on much longer than the previous day—for about two hours and a half. Fifteen to twenty minute periods of marching-chanting-singing were broken by sitting the troops down along the walls, giving them cold drinks and, once, taking them outside to cool off. Four, several staff people stood between the moving lines, dancing, gesturing the retarded to sing louder, and playing instruments.

The flex ended just before 3:00 p.m. and with the announcement that the mayor of San Francisco was at that moment on the phone with the Governor and had requested 15 minutes of silence while they talked. Further, the mayor said they would likely get a favorable decision and get it by 6:00 p.m.

The day-trippers were leaving rapidly and by 4:00 p.m. the protest was down to its elite of some forty persons, a minority of whom were disabled.

There was a lull and just before 4:00 p.m. the Secretary appeared, unexpectedly, and in a quiet voice and demeanor reported that he had studied all the material and that he supported the continuation of "all existing programs" but that was all he could do. He did not make the final decision. He left and the leaders and staff grimly commented among themselves that after all their effort with him, he turned out to be "just a flunky."

The leaders held a strategy meeting at 4:00 p.m. and it was quite striking that they did not talk about what they were going to do the rest of the day or about the fact that they were not talking about their not talking about the rest of the day. Rather, they involved themselves in thinking about pressuring officials the next day and in the coming weeks. Although no one said it outright, the decision had been made, de facto and unspoken, that they had run out of options in the current situation. The die had been cast and, further, they had heard a rumor the Governor was going to give them about 12 million dollars. How long to stay this day and what to do were left unaddressed.

Again a lull. Leaders, staff and handicapped were scattered on the premises; some in the reception room; others in the halls; yet others lounging on the Capitol lawn. Just past 6:00 p.m., a plainclothes assistant to the State Police Commander appeared at the reception room and announced he was going to lock its doors. Astonished, leaders present asked why and were told they had broken the rule about equipment. Accusations and counter accusations ensued. An odd new consideration was introduced by the Officer: He was concerned about unofficial people hanging about in the demonstration that made for security complications. This demonstration had had at least two unwanted and unknown "volunteers," one of whom had been taken into medical custody the previous day. A leader agreed to report any strangers and the officer then agreed not to lock the reception room doors. That was the end of the episode.

Again lull. Now and again, staff and disabled sang. They played board games, whiling away the time. What to do? The dinner hour passed in indecision and in the vague expectation that a certain aide to the Secretary (who was sympathetic to them) might come by and tell them the fate of the 18.9 million. Just before 9 p.m. leaders and staff brought themselves to talk about their situation and made the decision to stay until midnight, the time by which the Governor had, by law, to "sign the budget." Most of this talk, however, addressed long term questions of pressure, a tacit acknowledgement that this effort had, in a significant sense, already ended.

The door to the Capitol was locked at 9:00 p.m. Anyone leaving the building could not now return. It was three hours to midnight under the fluorescent lights of the reception room and in the now deserted, tomb-like and echoing marble hallways. Staff again sang sporadically, using new and humorous ditties, take offs on familiar songs, such as "[Governor's name, repeated] Are you sleeping? Are you sleeping?" to the tune of "Frere Jacques". And they watched as reporters were let into the Governor's complex to receive news of the budget. That is, the Governor was waiting until the last minute to make his budget decisions and would announce them at midnight.

Just past 11:00 p.m. someone modified the lyrics of "ninety-nine bottles of beer on the wall" to "fifty-five minutes of time on the wall" and a few people sang it. Two leaders immediately became alert to this and motioned for everyone to join in. The singing went on for some twenty minutes, using each successive number as the minute hand pointed to it on the pendulum clock that hung over the reception room door.

The lyric was counterpunctuated with the chant "[Governor's nick and last name] sign it now."

But as the minutes went on, the tempo and emotional energy of the singing built almost to a frenzy, accompanied by the thunderous beating of a wastebasket bottom and playing of instruments.

Then, at twenty-some minutes before midnight a new phase started. The young staff persons spontaneously formed into two teams of nine or ten each and performed a physical stunt every other minute, each. While one was performing for one minute, the other huddled and invented and planned its group stunt for the next minute. As group leaders of the handicapped, they were of course familiar with routines of play and performance. Among these stunts were mock battles in which female staff sitting on the shoulder of male staff fought in gladiator style. These activities were strenuous and as midnight approached, the participants seemed trance-like and on the edge of exhaustion.

Then it was midnight. Citizen Advocate and other leaders motioned for complete silence. Someone started to sing the song "the party's over..." but was "shhhed" into silence, as were other such bids for a definition of the situation. Everyone was motionless and silent for many moments, frozen and quiet for what seemed a long time. Softly, someone began humming, "We Shall Overcome," a humming that the group took up quickly. Citizen Advocate motioned for everyone to stand, form a circle, and join hands. While a staffer gently strummed a guitar and bodies swayed slowly, in unison, they continued to hum "We Shall Overcome." Tears streamed down many cheeks.

Still humming, the circle finally broke and the group began to file out, staff assisting the disabled and picking up equipment. One handicapped man broke into loud sobbing and crying made conspicuous by everyone else's silence. As they moved slowly down the hallway, a reporter came trotting by on his way to his paper and shouted to a leader "you got 13.8." There was virtually no response.

Four vans were brought to the Capitol North doors and loaded by staff. The leaders went separate ways. Citizen Advocate strode alone into the darkness. All the leaders and two of the vans had left when the sympathetic aide to the Secretary arrived to explain the budget action. Remaining staff turned their backs on him and one spat "screw you" at him.

As a parting gesture, a sign reading "Sign the Bill Now, Maintain the Centers" was left leaning against a tree by the Capitol North doors.

Spirited sieges tended, then, to relatively high levels of "flex" and strove to get their demands granted while the demanders were still on the scene. Both terminated with less than joyful compromise offers that each was more or less forced to accept. In the former, the leader stressed the gains made despite defeat on the item at immediate issue. In the latter, defeat was experienced and withdrawal achieved by means of an intensely expressive ceremony of tension release.

CHAPTER VII

LONG TERM VIGILS

Three episodes in the six year series were designed at the outset to last "as long as necessary" to achieve their respective goals and in fact each endured well beyond the relatively short bursts documented in the preceding chapter. The first, the Network Against Psychiatric Assault (NAPA), lasted twenty-nine nights; the second, the United Farmworkers (UFW) went fifteen nights; and the third, People United Against Rancho Seco (PUARS) persisted thirty-seven nights (see further, Chapter II, Section C).

We refer to these episodes as "vigils" in part because people prominent in the two we observed (the UFW and PUARS) themselves used that term in describing their activity, a use they adopted from a protest tradition in which it refers to "people remaining at a particular place as a means of expressing a point of view" over, first, a relatively longer period of time than many other modes of protest that is, second, "associated with a more solemn attitude" (Sharp, 1973:147). Regarding longevity, the illustrations provided by Gene Sharp (1973:147-148) in his treatment of the technique ran on the order of "weeks" and one ran a year.

Relative longevity and solemnity, or at least "subduedness" are likewise features of the two vigils we observed and is reported to have been true of the one that we did not (NAPA). "Relative" means precisely that, however, for, as we shall soon see, the UFW and PUARC vigils were not without some moments of "flex" as we have used that term in preceding chapters.

The sheer longevity of the UFW and PUARS vigils combined with the respective sequence of official responses kept changing the situation of the vigilers in decisive ways that provided turning points and formed "periods" within each that are much more clear than in the events we have examined until now. Accordingly, we have divided each into its main phases, phases formed more by the actions of officials than by the strategizing of the protesters. Indeed, here as in the other patterns, the extent to which officials, rather than protesters, structured the situation is impressive. Although the protesters had the initiative in "making an issue" it was the officials who selected and played the tune to which the protesters danced. Let us examine this first for the case of the United Farm Workers.

A. THE UNITED FARM WORKERS VIGIL

Toward the end of February, 1977, the Agricultural Labor Relations Board (ALRB) ruled that a certain non-United Farm Workers union could appear on the ballot of a representation election to be held March 3 at the Royal Packing Company in the Imperial Valley of California. The United Farm Workers argued that the particular union was a "company" one and demanded it be removed from the election ballot.

UFW people made their displeasure known at the El Centro ALRB office and on March 1 twenty-four of them were arrested on the complaint of the ALRB Chief Counsel for alleged disorderly behavior. UFW people counterclaimed that their conduct at the El Centro office was "completely peaceful" while the Counsel insisted they were threatening the workers and disrupting the office. This incident thus set in motion a sixteen day episode running from Wednesday, March 2 through Wednesday, March 16. The union instituted "vigils" at several ALRB offices, including the headquarters office at the Capitol, which was also the working office of the UFW nemesis, the Counsel himself. The headquarters office was on the third floor of Office Building Number One ("OB1"), a building located directly across the street from the Capitol. Access to ALRB quarters was through a single door opening onto a some fifteen by six foot waiting area containing four chairs. This small space was formed by three walls and a waist high counter beyond which there were several desks and associated equipment of ALRB secretaries. A tiny space, it was the immediate focus of the vigil. Outside the office was a forty by forty foot "lobby" with marble walls and floor topped by a ten foot high, fluorescent lighted ceiling. Otherwise bare, it was a very "hard space" and most of the crowd action of the occupation took place in it. (Not many months previously, ALRB headquarters had been in an office complex in suburban Sacramento, one that also housed dentists, doctors, and the like, people who had, in the past, complained about demonstrations directed against the ALRB. In relocating, an "informed source" of the Sacramento Union [1977] claimed that "security" had been a prime interest. It was easier to "keep track of demonstrations...and seal off the entrances...." in "OB1.")

The sixteen day UFW vigil was a single episode in the sense that 1) leading participants conceived it as such, 2) it was geared primarily to the issue of company unions, and 3) it went forth in a relatively sustained fashion. However, there were also significant variations within the episode in levels of mobilization and types of participants that enacted each of the phases.

1. FIRST FLUSH ANGER. The initial phase of "first flush anger" extended from Wednesday, March 2, the first mobilized day after the arrests, through Sunday, March 6. Its features were a spirited and relatively large gathering in the marble third floor lobby that tapered off through the day, dropped down to a core on Thursday, and with no on-site action on Friday, Saturday or Sunday.

The first flush of anger on Wednesday morning consisted of some thirty people, heavily young and Anglo supporters of farmworkers (rather than farmworkers), a few of whom occupied the waiting room chairs but most of whom stood about the marble lobby frequently being led (with guitar and hand clapping accompaniment) in songs such as "We Shall Overcome." Uniformed state policemen were in ample evidence, including some fairly high ranking ones who did not ordinarily appear at pickets, rallys or other protest occupations. Crowd size dwindled through the day down to a core half a dozen or so at 5:30 p.m. at which time this small group, led by UFW lobby staff persons, elected to sit-in overnight, an option that State Police had said they could exercise without fear of arrest or other such difficulty.

The next morning, about a dozen people, heavily Anglo UFW staff and other non-farmworkers, appeared at the office to talk with the Counsel, who, coming out of the reception area, offered to speak with a few but not the entire group in his private office. As was fairly common in situations of official-protester contacts, the group's leaders declined to split their people (and thus clearly to single out leaders) and asked to speak right there in the small waiting area and lobby. The Counsel consented. He explained why he felt the union in question was not a company creature. As the exchanges went on, the range of topics broadened and personal accusations were introduced. One person accused the Counsel of holding his job only for the money, a suggestion over which the Counsel bristled and retorted he had taken a substantial cut in income to assume his current post. Both sides became increasingly testy but the escalation of verbal heat seemed retarded by the constant necessity to pause and translate into Spanish for several of the participants. Also, in the group was a mid-twenties white male who adopted the classic "angry young radical" stance and who, among other things, asserted that the Counsel might well have the present group arrested on false charges right there and then, as he had allegedly done with people in El Centro a few days ago.

Exchanges continued inconclusively and the Counsel finally excused himself and started out of the building, walking very fast. The small crowd, carrying several dramatically red and black UFW flags on poles, tried to walk and talk with him but he outdistanced most and, finally, all of them were left behind in a block-long trail. That was the end of the action for phase one.

2. RALLY CROWDS. But phase two was in the wings. The organizing efforts of the Anglo, college-age lobbying staff turned to staging a "Demonstration of Solidarity" at noon, Monday, the seventh, an event said to "mark the continuation of the farm workers Vigil for Justice." It had perhaps become all the more critical to push ahead because the alleged company union had won over the UFW in the election held on Thursday, March 3.

Monday morning, more than a hundred people who seemed, indeed, actually to be farmworkers appeared in the marble lobby. Milling and standing about and often being led in singing and clapping, almost all the speaking was in Spanish. While definitely working class in dress and Hispanic in ethnicity, the crowd was highly mixed in sex and age. There were many small children and elderly people along with young and mature adults. (More ordinarily, Capitol protest crowds were decidedly homogeneous in composition.) As the time moved toward noon, the number of Anglo, middle-class supporters present slowly increased (many of whom were sympathetic state workers taking early lunches). Various picket signs, sans handles, leaned against the walls, declaring, for example, "ALRB UNFAIR TO UNION."

Earlier in the day the ALRB Counsel had agreed to "come out" and meet with the crowd in the marble lobby at 11:00 a.m. By about 10:30 a.m. the crowd, arrayed several people deep along the walls leaving the center of the lobby space bare, was called to attention by a tall and distinguished appearing black man in his thirties who we may refer to as the Leader. Although he seemed to speak little or no Spanish, he had been with the UFW for many years and according to one study of the union was among its perhaps five or six most important figures (Levy, 1975). He apprised the crowd that the Counsel was about to appear and quietly advised, through a translator, that

> We want to be polite to [The Counsel] but
> not to the point we are passive and let him
> talk down to us. We are men and women and
> we are here to talk to him and we want him
> to treat us like men and women.

Further, "we got the right to be here" and "we are going to stay here all night together" and until they, the workers, got appropriate answers to their questions about company unions. The situation thusly defined, a young, Anglo staffer led the crowd in songs until the Counsel appeared.

The interaction between him and the crowd took the form of answering questions and after a series of them on company unions, a rather different question was raised: What about certification of an election that was held some time ago in the Napa Valley, the nearby place from which the farmworker crowd now there in the lobby had come and the topic of concern over which had brought them there that day. The Counsel elected to go at that very moment and find out. While away, the Leader warned the crowd that the Counsel was likely to return with the certification in order to get rid of them. They had to be careful not to allow the Counsel to "divide the workers" in that manner. More singing and clapping ensued and the Counsel shortly returned with the positive news of certification and the announcement that at 9:00 a.m. the next morning, Tuesday, he would be able to provide the official document so stating. The Napa Valley farmworkers responded with elated cheers.

It was now almost noon and the crowd continued to increase in size as numerous sympathetic state workers arrived. Standing and milling in the almost jam-packed marble lobby, UFW staffers "warmed up" the crowd by leading it in the singing of spirited songs such as "We Shall Overcome" (in Spanish and English) and "We Shall Not Be Moved." Rhythmic clapping accompanied the singing. Several media crews drifted in, using bright lights to film in the relatively dark lobby.

The rally proper began with a young staffer introducing the Leader who reported the sequence of the conflict, the institution of the vigil, and the determination to continue the vigil until the issue of company unions was settled. Moreover, the certification action of that morning raised new questions of why large numbers of certifications were being held up and suddenly that morning one is produced, seemingly because those particular workers were there. The Counsel, declared the Leader, was attempting to divide the workers in the North and the South of the state.

Three "solidarity speeches" followed, one from an organization of state college professors and one each from two members of the state Assembly. A staff member announced that a paper was circulating on which people could sign up for four hours of vigil work at a time (12-4; 4-8, etc.) and for the entire night. The last speaker was a Catholic priest who both prayed and delivered a sermon on how the "people who control society do not seek human values," but, nonetheless "human values belong to everyone." Finally, just before 1:00 p.m., the crowd was formed into two rings, one within the other, and the people in each ring linked by crossed arms and hand holding. The people in each swayed gently while singing a low-keyed solidarity song in Spanish. Thus ended, the crowd multi-nucleated and many began drifting out. By 2:00 p.m. the marble lobby was virtually deserted and the vigil was maintained by only a token half dozen, mostly UFW Anglo staff.

Just after 2:00 p.m. a small incident of low-level State Police harassment took place. A UFW staffer had set up a table on which books, pins and other UFW items were displayed and were apparently for sale. Although nothing was actually sold, a police officer witnessed an offer to sell and thereupon wrote out a citation for violating state law. (This was in contrast to numerous other situations we observed in which State Police ignored solicitations or simply told people to stop it and did not issue citations.)

Monday night, on the order of twenty people slept over in the lobby and on the couches of the adjacent employee lounge. Most were Napa Valley farmworkers waiting for their certification from the Counsel at 9:00 a.m. the next morning. Among the sleep-overs was a famous Native American activist and his entourage. Plainclothes state policemen sat, in shifts, in the ALRB office; the door stood open and a ten day vigil candle sat lighted on the waiting room counter.

For whatever reason, the janitorial staff had not cleaned the marble lobby floor and by Tuesday morning it had become quite dirty. Crushed cigarette butts were especially evident.

Early in the morning the farmworkers began again to arrive in numbers and there were about 200 of them assembled shortly before 9:00 a.m. The Leader reminded them of the broader questions: Company unions and certification in general. The Napa Valley case was only one matter. And again:

> We want to be courteous to [the Counsel] but
> we don't want to sit here and act like kids so
> we want to ask him all the questions we have.

Six underlined police officers were quite visible at the edge of the lobby and in the adjacent hall.

The Counsel appeared, read the certification, and the crowd was virtually ecstatic. One of the farmworker leaders embraced the Counsel who thereupon departed quite quickly. This left the Leader with the problem of a satisfied farmworker crowd the members of which were likely to depart at any moment and would, in fact, all be gone before mid-day. He strove, though, to promote the larger and longer view to them and reminded them that vigils were going on in all seven of the ALRB offices around the state. The Counsel was not a hero; there were a great many problems to be solved. Starting this day, in fact, there were going to be delegations to meet with the Governor: "We are going to keep doing that day after day until we get the Governor to take some action." The Leader also announced that they had a surprise for the Counsel that morning. When he had first come out into the lobby, the Leader had handed him a subpoena that named him a defendant in a two million dollar damage suite for violating UFW members' civil rights!

The Native American Activist, still present from the previous night, was introduced as "a very good friend and long time supporter." The Activist pledged "if you are here 100 days, I will be here 100 days." (He left soon afterwards that day and was not seen on the premises again.)

This meeting ended with singing and by 10:00 a.m. a third of the crowd had already drifted out; by noon it was down to about thirty-five and declined slowly through the afternoon.

Around 11:00 a.m., the State Police officer in charge of Capitol security appeared and quite conspicuously paced about the ALRB office, the lobby, and the adjacent employee lounge, signalling by posture that he was inspecting. Huddling with the Leader, the "rules" of the sit-in were "negotiated" and became more restrictive. Addressing the some fifty people then lounging about the lobby, the Leader emphasized that their fight was with the ALRB and not the security of the building and they would abide by the new rules that the building would be locked at 5:30 p.m. and anyone there at that time could stay the night but no one new could come in and anyone leaving could not come back until the building opened in the morning. Stairs and elevators would not be blocked, there was to be no alcohol, no cooking, and the like. Further, the area would now be cleaned up by the building custodians.

Late in the morning, the Leader assembled a delegation of eight people, balanced between farmworkers and supporters, and announced to the sitting and standing group of now about forty people that the delegation would report back at noon the next day, Wednesday, on their success or lack of it with the Governor that afternoon and next morning.

At 2:00 p.m., the eight rather ceremoniously formed up in the marble lobby and walked the short block from the third floor of OB1 to the Governor's reception room. Two footpatrolmen and one motorscooter mounted state policeman monitored their walk. One officer accompanied them into the Capitol and another stood by in the hall as the delegation quietly occupied seats in the reception room.

It might be observed that the people ordinarily waiting in the reception room in order to enter the locked Governor's complex of offices were, in that season of the year at least, almost all dressed in upper middle class business attire. The males were commonly in three-piece suits. In contrast, the UFW delegation was outfitted in a combination of farmwork/outdoor garb and the late seventies "college scruffy" style. That is, they looked noticeably different from the ordinary users of the scene.

3. DELEGATIONS TO THE GOVERNOR. The initiation of formal rules for sitting-in in OB1 and the starting of delegations to the Governor's reception room marked the end of the second phase, which involved relatively large and rousing crowds and rallys, and the beginning of the third phase, a period of smaller groups who endured and carried on in a relaxed and low key fashion. In it, the day-time sit-in crew would sometimes be as few as three although it also sometimes briefly ballooned to as many as sixty when one or more groups of farmworkers arrived to do one or two four hour "stints." The overnight crew was relatively constant at ten persons or so. Moreover, actual farmworkers were in the minority most of the time in contrast to their majority in the brief second period. UFW staff and volunteers worked their established phone lists of supporters in the liberal and student communities in order to recruit people to do one or more four hour periods of service. As time went on, such supporters were noticeably day-tripping students of the University of California's campus at Berkeley, a place some seventy miles from Sacramento.

On Tuesday and Wednesday, the daily delegation to the Governor was conceived as likely to recur over a great many days. In forming up the delegation Wednesday, the Leader announced:

> Everybody is not going to go [today]. Some of the people are going to stay here to continue the vigil here....The people who don't go today [will get to go tomorrow and] will be doing the same thing tomorrow and the next day and the next day and everybody's going to have a chance to go meet with the Governor.

4.   QUIET VIGILING. But the delegation and the Leader returned that afternoon to report that while the vigil would continue, the delegations to the Governor were suspended. He had just talked by phone with the leader of the entire union, a man he referred to by his first name but who we may call the Great Leader, who had informed the Leader of his, the Great Leader's, phone conversation earlier that day with the Governor. The prime topic of their talk was an impending agreement with the Teamsters Union in which it would withdraw from organizing the farmworkers, and, thus, competing with the UFW. When the conversation was about to end, the Governor asked the Great Leader why some of his people were in the reception room waiting to see him. The Great Leader explained the issue of company unions to the Governor who responded that he was "ready to meet at any time." The upshot was an effort to arrange a meeting between the UFW attorney and the Governor. The delegations were therefore not needed. The vigil was to continue but the delegations would be stopped pending such a meeting.

Thursday through Sunday, March 10th through 13th, were uneventful. People came and went, the sit-in population varying between three and a couple of dozen. Sporadically, the group would sing and clap. There was quiet talking among cliques. Episodically, there were small "hassles" with the police, one or another of whom would suddenly ban various articles such as large pots, television sets and sleeping bags. A new ten day candle, the symbol of the vigil was lighted on Monday.

5. FINAL DELEGATIONS. A meeting between the UFW attorney and the Governor had not been arranged by Monday, March 14 and, in response, the delegations resumed that afternoon. Six members of it were still sitting in the Governor's reception room at 6:00 p.m. that day when the doors were to be locked. That is, the delegation elected to sit-in in the reception room past normal hours and the State Police retaliated by saying the delegation could stay but they were to be <u>locked in</u>. They could leave at any time, but they could <u>not</u> return, a rule that meant they had no access to toilet facilities. They left. Again Tuesday a delegation sat quietly waiting to see the Governor without success. And, finally, a singing and chanting delegation waited in the reception room on Wednesday afternoon.

That was the final and inglorious visit because UFW leaders decided Wednesday night to call off the vigil—to "pull back" and see how the Counsel responded over the next several weeks. As with so much in life, the episode did not end in a dramatic or definitive way. It simply stopped.

━━━━━━━━━━

This sixteen day sequence displays a long-term pattern of "flex and relax." Three relatively strong flexes are identifiable: the first flush of anger, the Monday morning rally, and the Tuesday morning reception of the certification notice. But overall, the effort was in relative repose and punctuated by only mild flexes, as in group singing and clapping in the Governor's reception room on the last day.

B. THE PEOPLE UNITED AGAINST RANCHO SECO VIGIL

The last significant protest occupation of the Governor's reception room was, ironically, also the longest and in many ways the most organizationally and social psychologically elaborate. After detailing the events, we will attempt to draw out some of the dynamics of this complexity.

1. STRATEGIZING AND STARTING (EARLY SEPTEMBER – NOVEMBER 29). In the early Fall of 1979, Northern California anti-nuclear groups held a series of regional meetings to discuss tactics for shutting down the Rancho Seco nuclear power plant near Sacramento. Attention was focused, in particular, on the Nuclear Regulatory Commission's (NRC) safety hearings on Rancho Seco scheduled for

November 28 in Sacramento.   These hearings seemed an auspicious occasion for the start of an action to close the plant.

In October and November, an action at the Governor's office was among tactics discussed in individual groups and at regional intergroup meetings. Other tactics included citizen's arrests of NRC members and the Governor, a mass walkout at the hearings, and civil disobedience at the plant itself.

October 13, an article that had an important impact on strategy discussions was published in the Sacramento Bee (Rennert, 1979).   It summarized an analysis made by the United States General Accounting Office to the effect that the more than eight million residents of northern California and Nevada would run the risk of excessive radiation exposure if the "worst possible" accident occurred at the Rancho Seco nuclear power plant.   In so estimating, the report enlarged the plant's "danger zone" to a 150 mile radius, thus encompassing the San Francisco Bay area on the west, Red Bluff, California on the north, Reno, Nevada on the east, and Fresno on the south. The scenario it pictured was based on the release of "substantial amounts of radioactive material following a hypothetical meltdown of Rancho Seco's reactor core and containment building." The report also pointed out that state and local governments did not have emergency plans covering all of the areas that would be affected in the worst possible accident. The significance of this article, from the emerging anti-nuclear coalition's perspective, was that there now existed documentation that a large number of people would be directly affected by a nuclear accident within their "home areas."   A much larger public therefore had a vital interest in closing the plant. The article thereby gave added impetus to the movement and would be featured in movement literature over subsequent months.

The strategy developed around the NRC hearings and from the above definition of peril consisted of three actions.   (1) A rally would be staged on the North Capitol lawn November 28, 1979, where it would be demanded that the Governor use his emergency powers to close the plant because it constituted "imminent peril" to citizens within the danger zone. (2) If no shutdown was ordered, the group would enter the Capitol and sit-in at the Governor's office.   (3) Civil disobedience would be undertaken at the plant itself involving a sit-in/blockade until the plant manager "grants our request to shut down the plant until proven safe."

The anti-nuclear posture just sketched and the three strategic actions and associated demands were communicated to aides of the Governor in a meeting with them on November 21, but to no effect. The plan needed, therefore, to be executed.

The purpose of the sit-in at the Governor's office was to bring the issue of emergency powers to shut down the plant to public attention and force the Governor to act.   It was the hope of some prospective participants that the non-violent demonstrators would be arrested and the action was, in part, planned with this aim in mind in order to make it a "test case" in the courts. However, other members of the group knew beforehand that if the protesters obeyed the rules for demonstrators in the office (no food or drink and no sleeping bags) they would not get arrested.

On the day of the rally, meetings were held between members of the group and representatives of the Governor. One group member, a young woman we will call Liaison, met that morning with the Commander of the Governor's security forces. She volunteered to be a liaison between the group and the State Police, stating that the imminent sit-in was to be non-violent and that the group wanted someone from the Governor's office to make a statement on the issue of Rancho Seco at the rally outside on the North lawn. As reported in an interview, she told the Commander: "If Governor Brown does not agree to shut down the plant, then we will stage a sit-in at his office. What time does the office close?" The Commander replied that the office closed at six o'clock. She then informed him that the group was planning to stay after that time. The Commander replied, "no you are not" and Liaison countered, "we are aware that we may be arrested, but this is something we must do," adding that the members of the group had nothing against the State Police "on a personal level." She also told him she wanted to speak with the Governor's energy aide. That aide was not available and Liaison went outside to the rally, returning after an hour to ask who from the Governor's office would make a statement at the rally. An aide answered that no one from the Governor's office would address the rally, but that she would have the opportunity to speak with the Governor's Chief of Staff later that day.

The young woman met again with the Commander, who informed her that the group now had permission to sit-in in the Governor's office, his position thus undergoing considerable change. Previously, the Commander had warned that they "may be arrested." But, although they would be allowed to stay, they would be locked in and not allowed to leave to use the bathroom. After some discussion the Commander also relented on this and said the group would have access to the bathrooms but could not unroll sleeping bags or bring food or drink into the reception room.

The rally ended in the early afternoon and about one hundred and fifty people crowded into the reception room and waited quietly for the outcome of the meeting, then being held in another room, between their leaders and the Governor's Chief of Staff.

At this meeting, leaders presented information about the dangers of Rancho Seco and asked the Governor's position on shutting the plant. Chief told the group that he could not speak for the Governor, who was out of town, but that he would be telephoning him soon and would ask.

Members answered "when you hear from the Governor, let us know—we will be out there [in the reception room] waiting." Chief responded that he might not hear anything until 9:30 that evening. They replied they did not care and that they would be waiting.

At this point people were, to quote one participant, simply "hanging out" and getting a sense of who would stay or leave that evening. Up until 9:00 p.m. some seventy-five people were present in the reception room but the number declined rapidly and about forty-five would actually stay overnight. The mood was characterized by several of the participants as being "the highest spirits of the whole action."

However, this mood was short-lived because conflicts over tactics also emerged that night. Several weeks prior to this rally and occupation, another action, that of civil disobedience at the Rancho Seco power plant, was planned. People intending to climb over the fence at Rancho Seco the next day (November 29) had set up a meeting at a location other than the Governor's office and were planning to leave the reception room at 9:00 p.m. in order to attend it. However, the majority of those present wanted everyone to stay together and not break into two separated groups. This marked the beginning of an ideological rift that appeared to coincide with geographical groupings. Those from Marin County anti-nuclear groups wanted to leave to attend the other meeting while those from Sonoma County wanted people to stay together in the Governor's office. The dispute was so sharp that some Marin people withdrew altogether and went back to Marin, deciding not to do the vigil or the civil disobedience at Rancho Seco.

There was a very tense meeting among the remainder over whether there would be civil disobedience at the plant or not. Among some there were feelings of panic and frustration over being unprepared for the next day's events. A few were outraged that necessary equipment, such as ladders, had not been secured. One subgroup held a "mini-non-violent training session" six hours before the action planned at Rancho Seco. The outcome of this chaotic state of affairs was that a small set of nine people would engage in civil disobedience Thursday, November 29.

By 9:30 the morning of that day, a press release had been drafted chastising the Chief for breaking his promise already to have communicated the Governor's answer to the group's "request" to close down the plant. It also stated that if the group did not hear from the Chief by 11:00 a.m. their statement would be released to the press. Sent to the Chief by means of the receptionist, within fifteen minutes the group was informed that a meeting with the Chief had been arranged for 1:30 p.m. that day. Timing was crucial for the contingent now at Rancho Seco (some twenty miles from the Capitol) who were preparing to climb the fence. If the Governor issued a shutdown order, the group would not "go over."

The meeting was scheduled to take place at 1:30 p.m. but the Chief kept them waiting half an hour. About thirty people were present for the ensuing two hour meeting in which he was given a list of complaints about Rancho Seco and a legal brief contending the Governor had the authority to close the plant. The Chief was noncommital during the meeting and afterwards told reporters only, "we are taking their concerns very seriously." Members of the group felt frustrated and left the meeting unsatisfied with the Chief's promise to talk with the Governor about their criticisms of the plant. "Our meeting got nowhere," one spokesman for the coalition told reporters.

Meanwhile, the protesters at the plant itself awaited word on the Governor's position. Calling to a pay phone near the East doors of the Capitol, one of them spoke with one of the reception room occupiers. Acting without knowledge of what the leaders were then discussing with the Chief, he told the protesters at the plant to climb the fence, saying simply, "go for it." They did so and were promptly arrested.

Even though otherwise non-commital, Chief did announce at the meeting that they could meet with the Governor himself on December 4th.

2. PREPARING TO PERSUADE THE GOVERNOR (NOVEMBER 29 - DECEMBER 4). The situation was now defined as requiring a detailed and persuasive presentation to the Governor and a set of "task forces" were organized and preparation for that meeting was the focus of efforts over the next four days.

There would eventually be twelve of these task forces which were essentially committees headed by a "coordinator" or "co-coordinator," people who were themselves "core members" of the effort (and whom we will describe shortly).

The immediate function of what seemed the four most central of the forces—the legal, medical, technical and moral—was to prepare arguments and presentations for the December 4th meeting with the Governor. That meeting, however, led to the even more important one of December 17th and these same task forces went forward to it, strengthened and augmented by eight additional "forces" that were evolving and also strengthened.

Among the four most central, the legal task force sought to establish that the Governor did, in fact, have authority under the Emergency Powers Act to close the plant. After the December 4th meeting it also attempted to locate more legal resources and to "organize legal opposition for coalition building." The medical task force concentrated on gathering evidence of the hazards of nuclear power plants to residents in the "danger zones" drawn around them. In expanded form for December 17th, effort was made to get noted anti-nuclear speakers and authorities to make presentations. A technical group researched the dangers of nuclear power and nuclear power plants and tried to establish that the plant constituted "imminent peril" to local residents. The moral task force, viewed by many as the most important, addressed questions of the cost to future generations if nuclear weapons and technology spread. It attempted to challenge the "business [and] government mentality that values profit over human health and life," and "would sacrifice children to keep business going," as one member described its function. For December 17th, its tasks included seeking the support/involvement of local churches, researching the "Nuremberg laws," and preparing other moral arguments against the use of nuclear power.

The eight other "forces" were a mixture of protest substance and protest maintenance and appeared in the following order on a sheet headed "TASK FORCES" that was drawn up and circulated. Labor sought "outreach to unions" and documentation of safety hazards at plants. Local Outreach was to "contact local groups," arrange a speakers' bureau and film showings, and distribute flyers, among other activities. Inreach aimed at increasing the participation of other anti-nuclear groups in the vigil. Media monitored "media response," drafted press releases, and acted as "Spokes People" for the press. Coalition Building was charged with "outreach to other environmental and progressive organizations." Alternative Energy focused on the conversion of Rancho Seco and questions of non-nuclear energy sources more generally. Clerical and Office was supposed to "keep all files," a scrapbook and (significantly) a "history and chronology," along with more ordinary clerical functions such as typing. Finally, the finance people were to "write checks," "keep track of the money," and engage in "fund raising."

So divided into specialized tasks, the group met as a whole, on strategy, twice a day, about 8:30 in the morning and about 7:30 at night. During these meetings, tactics of the protest, preparations for meetings with the Governor and his staff, and personal matters were discussed. People ordinarily sat in a closed circle on the reception room floor and on its "ratty" couches and chairs. During discussion, members often took notes, wrote letters and other communications, nursed babies, or strummed guitars softly.

Meetings were organized in terms of a "facilitator," a "notekeeper," and a "timekeeper." Usually these positions were filled on a volunteer basis in response to the question, "Who would like to facilitate, be timekeeper and take notes?" The role of the facilitator was critical. This person acted to keep the meeting flowing smoothly, called on people to speak, limited discussion, and made comments between participants' statements. Occupants of the position changed from meeting to meeting, although the more assertive and vocal members usually "facilitated." The notekeeper took notes in a red binder that was available to everyone for later reference.

After these positions were filled by volunteers, an agenda for the meeting was worked out. This was usually accomplished through a "stream of consciousness" dialogue between members who would state what they felt to be the pressing concerns of the group on that particular day. Each item on the agenda was weighted in importance by the assignment of a time limit—the most important items getting the most time.

Decision making was accomplished through "consensus." Every decision adopted had to have approval of all members present or at least the "non-dissent" of those who could not support a decision. In this and other ways, the meetings displayed the special form for which the anti-nuclear movement has become noted:

> Borrowing from the meeting process of the Quakers, decisions are reached by consensus, not by majority vote...Meetings take no action that is not consented to by every participant. If anyone dissents from a decision, discussion must continue until everyone consents to the proposal. Those who do not agree but do not feel strongly enough to block consensus may "stand aside" and allow the group to reach a decision despite the absence of total consensus. Since the decisions reached represent, per force, a compromise of views among all those present, the anti-nuclear alliances have intended consensus as a way of allowing all meeting participants to be involved in the making of decisions without anyone feeling coerced (Barkan, 1979:29).

The protesters were a coalition of activists drawn from anti-nuclear power groups in northern California. Most were members of "affinity groups"—local groups—in the North Coast counties of Marin, Mendocino, and Sonoma and were affiliated with the Abalone Alliance and an organization known as SoNoMore Atomics. At this point, their numerical strength on the premises during an ordinary day was between two dozen and a "hardcore thirty" (Witt, 1979). The group included a nurse, psychologist, graduate student, and several teachers, college students, "free spirits," countercultural "types," political activists, and theatrical performers. They ranged in age from ten to fifty-five (with the largest number in their twenties) and were nearly all white with an approximately even split between males and females.

They can be grouped into three distinct "strata" based on levels of commitment and participation. For a small nucleus or "core group" of protesters, numbering thirteen to fifteen, participation in the vigil was the almost total focus of their existence and involved a significant disruption of their personal lives. These individuals were present for all or most of its thirty-seven night duration and were frequent overnight occupiers. They were central to the vigil's organization—proposing courses of action and implementing them once they had passed consensus—and to its maintenance—coordinating and serving on the essential tasks forces. They also served as representatives of the group in meetings with members of the Administration, the Governor, the State Police in the Capitol Building, and the newspaper and television reporters covering events of the vigil.

Prominent figures in the core group were:

Mary, a frizzy haired woman in her late thirties, was the owner of a second-hand clothing establishment. Clad in counter-cultural garb—long skirts, peasant blouses, boots and colorful jewelry—she was one of the two or three most central figures. Vocal, assertive at times, "humanistic," always encouraging others to participate and trying to generate a "high level of energy" among the protesters, Mary was viewed by many as the "core of the core group."

Roger, a clinical psychologist in his mid-thirties, also played a key role. Bearded and casually dressed in sweaters, slacks and sandals, he was an important source of strategies and planning options and often acted as a facilitator at group meetings.

Larry, a nurse in his mid-twenties, was tall, dark complexioned with long mustache and hair. He frequently dressed in a hooded peasant shirt and loose fitting white pants and often dealt with reporters and Governor's aides and helped with organizational matters.

Don, a heavily bearded ex-social worker in his late twenties favored work shirts, jeans, heavy boots, and cap and played protest ballads and soothing melodies on his acoustic guitar throughout the vigil's course. He also was an important "input" into the group's decision making process.

White Cloud, a native American with long dark hair was a soft-spoken, eloquent public speaker, drawing from his theatrical training. He was a central figure in the group's plays and other presentations to the public and press and wrote and performed a one-man dramatic narration against nuclear power at the group's Christmas day celebration. He was also the focus of PUARS' post-vigil theatrical protest events.

The second, and largest, body of protesters, the "regular participants," some twenty in number, was in some flux. People would come and go depending on the amount of time they could devote. Thus, some individuals stayed for a week or more while others stayed for a day or series of days, leaving and then returning. Members of this strata also had differing levels of involvement in group activities. They served on the various task forces, organizing events, raising funds, and doing research. Along with core group members, they slept on the hardwood floor and on the furniture in the reception office, ate meals in the marbled corridors and on the outside steps of the Capitol Building, washed themselves in the building's bathrooms, and conducted their outside affairs through pay telephones. They sang anti-nuclear power songs, cared for their children who accompanied them, and exchanged personal and movement information with each other during lulls in the vigil.

The third strata in the vigil, amounting to perhaps 150 people, the "sporadic participants," limited their involvement to several hours up to a day or so. They were infrequently overnight occupiers and commuted from their homes to the vigil to attend events they were told would be significant. Included here are people in the crowds of activists and sympathizers who attended the outdoor rally on November 28 and those who packed the reception room on December 4th and 17th during meetings with the Governor on those days. Also a part of this strata were the several speakers and experts who testified before the Governor December 17th. While their participation in the day-to-day events of the vigil was minimal, their presentational involvement played an important part in the drama. The experts who testified on December 17th, in particular, legitimated and strengthened the group's position on the issues and made a more persuasive case, in the protesters' view. The crowds which packed the outer office boosted the morale of the regular and core protesters and were visible evidence that the group was not alone in its opposition to Rancho Seco's operation.

Resuming our narrative against this organizational and personnel background, the morning newspapers of Tuesday, December 4th reported the Governor as saying he would not meet with the protesters, contrary to the promise of the Chief. Reading this statement, the occupiers were angered and drafted a press release denouncing him as a "false friend of the anti-nuclear movement." A copy of it was given the receptionist and she was told it would be released to the press if the promised meeting did not take place.

Receiving this threat, Governor's aides hastily rescheduled the meeting. PUARS people felt this was significant because of the Governor's busy schedule—he was campaigning for President of the United States at the time and would only be in Sacramento for a brief period.

Twenty members met with him for an hour and a half that day. Sitting around the large table in the conference room adjoining the reception room, leaders stated the general purpose of the vigil and listed seven demands, including the key one of closing Rancho Seco. In discussion, he granted six but demurred on the seventh, closing Rancho

Seco. The six were: (1) issuing a public statement announcing the next meeting between himself and the group (which was set, at this meeting, for December 17th at 9:00 p.m., following an office party for his staff) at which time he would also disclose his position on the safety of Rancho Seco; (2) placing announcements in major Northern California newspapers publicizing safety hearings scheduled for February (the November 28 NRC hearings had been cancelled because of a member's illness); (3) permitting participation of the protesters in those hearings and providing open-ended time for public testimony; (4) giving assistance from his office and the State Energy Commission in gathering information for a shutdown of Rancho Seco; (5) involving the state in measuring radiation levels within Rancho Seco; and, (6) providing space in the Capitol building for the group's use in educating the public about Rancho Seco, nuclear power in general, and energy alternatives.

The exchange itself was informal and consisted largely of "free flowing dialogue" and a "give and take" between the two parties. One member of PUARS attempted to give a technical presentation on the health hazards of the plant to area residents, but was cut off due to time constraints.

Relative to pressure tactics, while the meeting was in progress, dozens of supporters who had come to the Capitol for the meeting were milling about in the reception area along with many news people and the amalgam of tourists and others who filled the Capitol halls at mid-day.

Even though the protesters received the Governor's promise that his administration would in some ways assist the group in its fight against nuclear power, they decided to maintain the vigil in the reception room in order to see that the concessions were implemented and to continue efforts to persuade him to use his emergency powers to shut Rancho Seco. Moreover, and as we will discuss below, there was a great deal of tension and suspicion between local anti-nuclearists and the PUARS people who came predominately from North Coast counties of California. Not trusting the local anti-nuclearists to press on and to monitor the concessions, PUARS people had all the more reason to remain on the scene.

In terms of the momentum and direction of the vigil, the most important result of the December 4th meeting was the Governor's agreement to meet with them again on December 17. This promise created another concrete time-place goal and framed PUARS activities over the next thirteen days, a sequence that formed a third phase of the vigil.

What we may think of as the ambiance, "atmosphere," or even culture of the vigil was also emerging with clarity by December 4th and would permeate the days to come. It was most visible and striking in terms of the physical items that protesters brought with them. In addition to the sleeping bags, backpacks, clothing, musical instruments and other personal effects that cluttered the office, PUARS members placed a variety of posters, charts, and signs about the room. Colorful posters with rainbows, stars, solar imagery, the PUARS logo, and phrases such as "No Nukes is Good Nukes," "Safe Enough is Not Safe," and "Hell No We Won't Glow" were conspicuous. One was even attached to the front of the receptionist's desk.

Posters were also displayed on a makeshift, cardboard literature table placed at the reception room door, a table that additionally contained anti-nuclear leaflets, bumper stickers, buttons, shirts, and other paraphernalia along with a series of petitions which would be sent to local, state, and federal officials asking support for the group's efforts and demanding action be taken to close down Rancho Seco and put a halt to the utilization of nuclear power.

Important both as culture and as organizational devices were several kinds of special placards. One was the "duty roster." Protest days were divided into two hours shifts and members were encouraged to sign up and "show up" for their assignments. (This tactic was utilized when protest numbers began to diminish, in late December, and the number of occupants dropped to a handful of people.) Another and earlier placard encouraged participants to sign up and serve on the various "task forces." Still another was employed to encourage the use of carpools because many "regular" and "sporadic" participants commuted from Sonoma and Marin counties, a distance of approximately one hundred miles. And yet another, described below, gave the "rules" of the vigil.

Also of cultural significance, many members, having limited resources and contacts in the Sacramento area, were forced to keep their children with them in the reception room. At several points during the vigil a half dozen infants were in attendance, crying, playing with toys, and/or crawling around on the office floor. Baby books, dolls, toys, and blankets were often strewn across the floor and on the furniture. Aged approximately two to six years old, they sometimes occupied themselves by playing tag and rearranging the furniture. The presence of children, while frequently annoying and disruptive, served, however, to offer a humorous diversion on numerous occasions, breaking up the tense atmosphere at critical points in the vigil's chronology.

The descriptions of key participants, provided above, and cultural themes such as these point, of course, to the special variety of "intellectual proletariat" that these anti-nuclearists constituted. It is a movement born of "the resettlement of urban intellectual workers...in the rural zones, a move largely stimulated by the various sixties movements" (Widmer, 1979:5).

3.   AGAIN PREPARING TO PERSUADE THE GOVERNOR (DECEMBER 4 - 17). In the third phase, task force activity increased, internal organization was elaborated, and outreach for monetary and moral support from the public and concerned organizations was undertaken.

Tasks for the vigil were discussed at a strategy meeting on December 5th. One person was assigned the job of creating a "rules board" that listed behavior prohibited by the State Police. Under the title "Fun Things to Do in the Governor's Office," the "rules" of the vigil were given: (1) no food or drink in the office; (2) sleeping bags could not be unrolled; (3) electrical appliances were not allowed. The role of "greeter" was created—an individual to distribute literature and talk with the interested public, tourists, and curiousity seekers. Fundraising tactics were discussed—options mentioned included selling "T"-shirts and bumper stickers, showing films, collecting business donations, and holding a dance. Local outreach tactics included the creation of a flyer listing the needs of the group and the construction of a mailing list.

An agenda for the meeting with the Chief scheduled for December 10 was also discussed. Items mentioned included the group offering to "process" relevant mail and telegrams coming into the Governor's office, to "be his secretary" in order to monitor public sentiment. Other important concerns to be presented to the Chief were storage of food and belongings and the physical hardships they had to endure. There were complaints about having to sleep under fluorescent lights that were left on twenty-four hours a day, some feeling that this was a purposeful tactic to make things difficult for them. There were also complaints about not being allowed to unroll sleeping bags and thus having to sleep on hardwood floors.

At the next morning's meeting, December 6, the character of the protesters' relationship to the Governor was considered and the group decided to stress "our working relationship" in press releases and literature. It was also decided that a minimum number of persons needed to be present in the reception room—at least three—at any given time.

Friday morning, December 7, several members visited a local elementary school and showed three films on the dangers of nucelar power ("The Medical Effects of Radiation," a film by Dr. Helen Caldicott, an anti-nuclear medical authority held in esteem by members of the group; "Lovejoy's Nuclear War;" and, "Danger: Radioactive Wastes"). Occasionally over subsequent days other "outreach" efforts of this kind were undertaken.

The evening meeting on December 8 was further devoted to specific task force planning. The legal task force would contact a local law school in an attempt to get advice on the issue of the Governor's emergency powers and help for those arrested at Rancho Seco the 29th of November. The moral task force would send a flyer to local churches and contact local religious leaders to speak on the "religious implications of nuclear energy." The labor task force was to coordinate a mailing campaign to labor organizations and give support to workers' rights in struggles with management.

The "coalition building" task force was to set up meetings with groups such as the Gray Panthers and the American Indian Movement along with contacting lesbian, gay, environmental and other "progressive" groups. The "alternative energy" task force was to do research on solar energy possibilities for home and industry usage. The "entertainment" task force (an entity not part of the more formal structure) would collect names of musicians, poets, and others who would perform and speak out against Rancho Seco and nuclear power and aid in fundraising. Also discussed was the creation of a poster with the caption, "If nuclear power plants are safe, why can't they be insured?"

The task forces reported their activities at a strategy meeting Sunday morning, December 9. The legal force was working on the "Emergency Powers Act presentation" for the December 17th meeting and arranging fine money for what were now called the "Rancho Seco 9." The possibility of a citizens' arrest of government officials was also discussed. The medical force reported the views of a woman who had dropped by the reception room from the previous day and provided information on how nutritionally to stave off radiation poisoning.

Monday, December 10 five protesters met with the Chief in order to begin implementing commitments made by the Governor at the December 4th meeting and a wide range of topics were treated at the group's strategy meeting that same day. First, there was "brainstorming" of ideas on what to present to the Governor. Major concerns included: the numbers of protesters who would meet with the Governor; the attitude they should take at the meeting (avoiding "blackmail"); the Governor's timetable and commitment; the need to have an attorney present; the importance of looking professional; making written vs. oral presentations; the possibility that the Governor did not need to be convinced, only a strong technical report and broad public backing was required; the Governor should not be the sole focus of their efforts.

Second, about fifteen minutes were spent brainstorming ideas for what to do after the meeting on December 17th if the Governor refused closure. One view advocated staying in the office to maintain pressure which would show they were not willing to give up on the Governor. Another view suggested moving the vigil close to the plant itself by finding a sympathetic farmer and creating a "tent village" on his land until the plant closed.

Third, task force members presented updates on their work. Significance was accorded the legal and moral committees' exploration of the "Nuremberg International Law question." The idea was that operators of the plant were morally bound to close it and could not claim they were just "following orders" should an accident occur. Fourth, the media committee was thinking about drafting a press release on what they felt to be the poor response by the Chief to requests for meetings and information.

Fifth, a local televison news commentator had brought them under a scathing attack, characterizing them as a "bunch of jobless, state-supported, unwashed hippies." Many felt it was important to answer what they saw as an untrue characterization. Some members proposed dressing a bit better while others felt that doing so would be presenting a false picture and was therefore wrong. (A few did in fact wear more presentable dresses, jackets and ties in subsequent days.) Later press releases and statements to the press included references to them being from "all walks of life" and claimed that none of the occupiers was on welfare. The responsible, middle class occupations of some occupiers were also mentioned, as in there being an attorney, business person, psychologist and several students in their ranks.

On December 15 the occupiers' work agenda included, first, creation of a short orientation statement to present people new to the vigil and to the public more generally. Second, "coalition building" was stressed. There was talk of (but little action on) approaching such groups as the Unitarian Church, the Gray Panthers, Greenpeace, the United Farm Workers, the Governor's Office of Appropriate Technology, the Union of Concerned Scientists, local Indian groups, the Sacramento Food Co-op, the Musicians United for Safe Energy (MUSE).

Third, the question of what to do after the December 17th meeting with the Governor was raised again. Suggestions under discussion and debate included: moving the vigil to the plant and seeking popular support for early 1980 hearings on the plant; assuming a firm working relationship with the Governor and maintaining a daily presence in the office to educate the public (not a full occupation); seeking a relationship with farmers near the plant in order to live there; continuing the vigil at the present location to "keep a hand on the pulse of power;" establishing contact with Rancho Seco employees to "feel them out;" and, blockading the plant.

Fourth, it was now decided to have thirty people at the December 17th meeting, including seven negotiators and two facilitators. Also under discussion were criteria for the selection of those to attend. Should these be people who had worked on the task forces and/or who have put in the most time? Did the act of sleeping over symbolize a high level of commitment?

On Sunday, December 16 there was a marked increase in the number of participants, supporters, and sympathizers who planned to stay for the meeting with the Governor the next day, an increase from about thirty to about one hundred and fifty people. There was much showing of emotion as people from the various member groups of the coalition hugged and kissed one another in greeting. The evening strategy meeting this day was devoted almost entirely to the imminent meeting with the Governor. Topics discussed included the need to look "professional," and make "tight" presentations. The content and order of presentations and meeting logistics (e.g. who would sit where) were considered. The tentative agenda consisted of: (1) an introductory statement emphasizing that the goal of the group and purpose of the vigil was the "shutdown of Rancho Seco;" (2) the showing of a thirty-eight minute film on the dangers of nuclear power; (3) presentations by "experts" secured by the coalition, giving evidence for the plant's closure. The intention was, moreover, to keep the meeting from being too "businesslike." The actual order of agenda items was to be emergent and left to the discretion of the seven negotiators.

Options and strategy for after the 17th were discussed once again at this meeting and viewpoints on the length and goals of the vigil were aired. Loss of support by people leaving for the holidays in late December was of concern but it was also argued that the energy level of members was incredibly high at this time. That fact would insure sufficient levels of the commitment, focus and energy needed to keep the pressure on. A proposal to stay indefinitely in the Governor's office unless the plant was shut was "tested for consensus" and passed. A sign-up poster for a minimum number of people to stay each day through Christmas was drawn up and passed around.

At the morning meeting of December 17 the team of seven negotiators was selected by the usual method of consensus. Those selected, however, were primarily the "core" protesters (described above), the people who had maintained a "constant presence" in the Governor's office and coordinated the various task forces. Also finalized were the numbers of speakers to present evidence at the meeting: two legal, one medical, two alternative energy, two technical, one moral, one labor. Thirteen "silent participants" plus two alternates were, additionally, to be included. They would be selected on the basis of their commitment to the vigil as evidenced by time spent and work performed. Their role would be to sit in the back of the room and act as witnesses to the events. They could, moreover, communicate by written notes with the negotiators or facilitators, offering ideas, suggestions, and needed information. They would, further, "focus energy and send it out," and give feedback afterwards.

At a 6:00 p.m. meeting of negotiators and presenters a final agenda and order of presentation was worked out for the 9:00 p.m. meeting and presenters publicly rehearsed their talks. The crowd formed a large circle in the packed reception room, presenters introduced themselves to the group and ran through the areas they would speak on that evening. People commented, agreed, or asked for modification of the content of each's presentation

Also about this time a silent participant selection meeting was held in the hallway near the Capitol East entrance and in front of the bank of phone booths. With the sound of ringing phones in the background and members jumping up to answer them, the thirteen silent participants' roster was finalized.

In the early evening the "energy level," as the protesters termed it, was extremely high—quite possibly the highest of the vigil. Indicating such a high level were frequent reunion huggings, group singing of rousing anti-nuclear songs, sharing of food between strangers, and participants' frequent exclamations to one another that the "energy level" was, indeed, high.

At 9:00 p.m., the time set for the meeting, the reception room was packed with people and they were flowing out of the office and into the hallway. At the peak of the evening, there were more than 200 clustering and milling about and the overall scene was reminiscent of a large "cocktail party." People in the hallway were talking, laughing, smoking cigarettes, strumming guitars, and playing various board games. Some were sleeping, meditating, chanting, or simply "hanging out."

The Governor kept the group waiting three hours past the scheduled 9:00 p.m. and people grew visibly tired, frustrated, and angry as the evening progressed. Several segments of the crowd attempted to lift spirits by singing songs and engaging in theatrical performances. One young man put on a "Tricky Dicky" Nixon mask and went from cluster to cluster of people trying to make them laugh.

The meeting itself finally started at midnight and lasted two and one-half hours. The Governor and his staff listened patiently to the presentations by the task force leaders and the outside experts. These latter included a member of Physicians for Social Responsibility who presented medical arguments against nuclear power; the director of the Northern California Ecumenical Council who made an anti-nuclear appeal on moral grounds; a graduate student at a local university, who highlighted the technical limitations of Rancho Seco, and the dangers these limitations posed for the public; and, a state university physics professor who testified that, contrary to what nuclear power advocates claimed, operators of Rancho Seco were not "scientists" and the plant had no minimum educational requirements for its reactor operators. A person from a Catholic Senior Citizens' Center addressed the issue of the production of bio-mass and alcohol fuels—one means of converting nuclear power plants. A labor organizer spoke about the relation of unions and workers to nuclear power production and of "an increasingly clear labor movement against nuclear power." A member of the Solar Program at the Farallones Institute talked about retrofit solar water heaters and advocated a well funded educational system on alternative energy sources.   An engineer analyzed the conversion of Rancho Seco.   A recent law school graduate articulated legal issues associated with the controversy.   The moral implications of allowing the plant to continue operation were highlighted by a core member of the group and he made a direct appeal to the Governor to use his conscience in this matter.   A film that antinuclearists thought was particularly persuasive on the anti-nuclear issue, "The Medical Implications of Nuclear Energy," was shown.

The Governor did not change his position and continued to maintain that he did not possess the authority to close the plant.   It was by now almost 3:00 a.m. and all parties were quite tired.   The meeting quietly ended.

4. DEMORALIZATION AND REDUCED DEMANDS (DECEMBER 18 – 24).   Receiving no commitment to close the plant, the next morning and the next several days, the occupiers debated the "pro's and con's" of continuing their vigil at the Governor's office.   Those arguing for a continued presence cited diverse reasons.   (1) Media coverage was easier to get.   (2) The location was good for forming "outreach" connections to other groups.   (3) The particular location "furthers our determination to shut down the plant."   (4) The political character of the place "teaches how to deal with government and media."   (5) It is easier to have the entire families of supporters present.   (6) The government would be forced to make a stand if they decided to launch civil disobedience (such as blockading the office).

Those arguing for a shift in tactics cited "negative aspects" of the setting.   (1) The environment was not "conducive to group process." There were many visual and auditory distractions and concentration was hard during meetings.   (2) It was difficult to sleep on hardwood floors and eat in hallways and outdoors. (3) The location of the vigil might be alienating "possible new members or coalitions." (4) The reception room might not be the most practical or efficient place from which to inform the public of the issue. (5) The physical focus of the group was too narrow.   People should go to other sites and protest.   (6) The constant flow of new people into and out of the setting made it difficult to get things accomplished; there was a chronic "orientation problem" that slowed down the progress of the group.

The meeting of late Tuesday, December 18 was emotionally charged and a great deal of weariness, frustration, hurt, and anger were displayed as alternatives were debated.   Major proposed lines of action were: (1) extending the vigil to a specific date such as Christmas Day; (2) ending the vigil immediately for a specific reason and having "clarity to and control of the ending;" (3) increasing activity—holding another rally and blockading the plant; (4) finding a house in Sacramento to live in while the vigil continued; (5) launching "mass actions" such as door-to-door canvassing in the Rancho Seco 150-mile "danger zone."

Failing to achieve consensus on a course of action the protesters simply continued the vigil. Complaints about the physical inconveniences associated with the occupation increased. Sleeping on the hardwood floor, eating meals on the steps of the Capitol in cold and rainy weather, personal affairs at home left unattended, and twenty-four hour exposure to fluorescent lights all seemed to be taking their toll on the some twenty people who were persisting.

Indeed, the occupation began and ran on quite minimal coalitional as well as personal resources. This fact was itself in significant part responsible for the heaviness of the toll being taken. On the coalitional side, for example, some of the occupiers we have described in previous chapters had sufficient political friends in the Capitol building (and in Sacramento) that phones could be used free and even offices slept in (see, e.g. the account of the Title XX coalition in Chapter VI). For phones, PUARS was even reduced to using the bank of public ones standing near the Capitol East doors (and those were the numbers listed on their press releases.) Some funding came from the larger anti-nuclear groups making up the coalition that was PUARS, but this was insufficient. Perhaps most critical, the leaders and members in the largest anti-nuclear groups in the immediate vicinity—the Sacramento Valley—were not sympathetic to the tactic of a vigil in the Governor's office and were quite suspicious of PUARS, some spokespeople characterizing them as "wackos," "off the wall," "loonies," and "outrageous" (Barnes, 1980). Speculating that they might "actually be agents for the other side" because they "hurt" the "legitimate anti-nuclear movement," members of local groups in fact tried to "keep other organizations from helping [PUARS]... with funding" (Barnes, 1980).

At the start (and before collective food purchasing evolved), a hat or other container was passed and a few people went to local food stores, returning with filled arms and greeted with rousing cheers. In addition, food and donations were sought from sympathetic individuals and groups in Sacramento. Local health food stores and cooperatives sent fruit and baked goods. Lodging was extended by other, local sympathizers and by vigilers who lived within commuting distance. This hospitality proved invaluable; the core "around the clockers" were much in need of a change of scenery, a comfortable bed, hot shower, and a quiet environment.

On the more personal side, the core protesters were plagued with financial difficulties. Many had interrupted their daily routines and their incomes were drastically reduced or halted. By mid-January, one core occupier resorted to sending an emotional, xeroxed letter to her friends soliciting support. Reporting that three of the occupiers had lost jobs because they were away from their work too much, she appealed for money to support PUARS and her personally since she had not been able adequately to attend to her second hand shop located in a Sonoma County city.

Two emerging themes of the group meetings after December 17 are of special note. One, as mentioned, several people urged "mass outreach" by which was meant door-to-door canvassing and other "on the ground" forms of leafleting and contact. Two, more talk was devoted to ordinary lobbying of the legislature. Names of legislative committees, their chairs and members, were assembled. Who might best be approached was debated. Most notable about this line of talk was the protesters' ignorance of the structure of the political process at the Capitol and the names of the key "players" in that "game."   Neither of these conversational concerns was acted on in significant ways, however. Moreover, these emerging topics combined with modest efforts at coalition with comparatively marginal and small social movements (e.g. the American Indian Movement) and did not stress the larger and local anti-nuclear organizations. Taken together with the effort directly to pressure the Governor, these made up a relatively restricted strategic vision.   Despite the fact, for example, that they were within a few hundred yards of an office of each of the major (and "establishment") as well as minor interest groups of California (and of American society), these resources were barely discussed much less sought out as sources of support.

At the evening meeting of Friday, December 21 there was serious talk of leaving. One leading member declared "the vigil is falling apart" and suggested "let's end on a bright note; let's get an 8 to 5 office and house."   Another suggested negotiations with the Chief to obtain some concessions before leaving, a suggestion that was taken up as the operating goal of the group and occupied subsequent meetings.

The morning strategy meeting on December 24 was devoted to preparing to meet with the Chief later that day. Three negotiators and five alternates were "consensed." The demands developed were calculated in terms of what the Administration might reasonably do "to further our mutual goals." The four main ones were: (1) providing a table for the group's literature in the reception room; (2) arranging for anti-nuclear films to be shown in three major cities in California; (3) allowing special input into the Office of Emergency Services (OES) hearings on the safety of Rancho Seco, now scheduled for January 26, 1980; (4) assistance in investigating State Employee Pension Funds, some of which were allegedly invested in the nuclear industry.

The Chief met with the group in the reception room for two hours on Christmas Eve. Stating they were prepared to remain until these demands were accepted; they thus made a key retreat from the prior vow to stay until Rancho Seco was closed.   The Chief granted the demands in principle and a January 2 meeting was arranged in order to finalize them.

The occupiers held a public celebration of Christmas on December 25. A large and colorfully decorated Christmas tree located near the East doors of the Capitol (a seasonal display unrelated to the protesters) provided an impressive backdrop for what was a true "media event." Summoned by press release, local television and newspaper people covered the scene in which some forty spectators and performers put on a program, lasting about an hour, consisting of anti-nuclear skits, songs, and speeches. Visiting protesters brought home-cooked "organic food" and there were various baked goods. The atmosphere was one of festivity and many said it was a welcome break from the rigors of the vigil.

5. SETTLEMENT, WITHDRAWAL, DEMISE (JANUARY 2 - EARLY MAY).

At the meeting of January 2, the Governor's Aide on energy matters agreed to help the group prepare for the OES hearings, to arrange showings of anti-nuclear films in Los Angeles, San Francisco, and Sacramento; to provide space for public anti-nuclear presentations; to investigate the State Employee Pension Funds; and to arrange for a table in the reception room where the group could dispense literature on the dangers of Rancho Seco.

The energy aide also told the group that the Governor's administration was supportive of the protesters' efforts to close the plant but when the Governor left the state, as he was now doing frequently in his run for President of the United States, the Lt. Governor assumed control of the government. He stressed that the Lt. Governor and the conservative legislature, soon to reconvene, might attempt to evict the protesters by force if necessary. He suggested they place "sacred documents," such as the Bible and the U.S. and California Constitutions, under and mixed in with the group's own literature. This would serve to make the Lt. Governor look like a villain should he order the table thrown out of the reception during a period the Governor was out of the state.

All the scaled down demands having now been met, the group prepared to end the vigil. An anonymous contribution of $1,000 came in at this time and this money allowed a dozen core members to stay in a nearby hotel while seeking a more permanent location from which to organize a day-time only presence in the reception room.

They moved their personal effects from the reception room the evening of January 3, accomplishing the task in only fifteen or so minutes. The accumulated melange of boxes full of literature, makeshift cardboard tables, sleeping bags, clothing, books, baby blankets, and toys were carted out with swiftness and efficiency. Almost immediately the custodial staff arrived to clean up the room and the places where protesters' artifacts had stood.

Next day's PUARS press release, January 4, announced the change of "action" at the Capitol:

> PUARS...will maintain a presence in the State Capitol, continuing to inform the public about the dangers of nuclear power. For our public education campaign we will distribute literature and answer questions from visitors during regular business hours at the Capitol...Our ongoing dialog with the...Administration has been productive in finding shared goals and strategies. We thank those groups and individuals who have joined us during the past 38 days. [PUARS] is planning to open an office in the Sacramento Community in order to continue working toward the closure of Rancho Seco.

Over subsequent weeks, the number of protesters ordinarily present in the reception room dwindled down from seven or eight to one or two and, into April, none a good deal of the time. Governor's staff and visitors again became the most conspicuous persons in the reception room. On one occasion, a protester was asked by the receptionist if he was in fact "one of the protesters" because she was "keeping track of the protest" and had the impression no one from the group was present at that time. Tourists also stopped and asked which, if any, individuals were a part of the protest.

In addition to maintaining the literature table and staffing it during office hours in January and February, PUARS people showed anti-nuclear films in several cities, conducted six "teach-ins" in the Sacramento area (using an auditorium provided by the state), and prepared for the safety hearings on Rancho Seco to be held by the State Office of Emergency Services.

The weekend of January 19th the dozen die-hards began work on an office located a few blocks from the Capitol. Members lived in a loft built in the back of the space and continued activities from there.

Into late April, the staffing of the literature table was increasingly sporadic. By early May no one was appearing and the literature on the table gradually disappeared; finally it stood empty. Having no purpose, workers removed it from the reception room.

About the same time, the office-sleeping quarters of the protesters closed and the core members scattered for other pursuits. One of them enrolled for training at a wholistic health institute. Another took a job as a dishwasher in a cooperative restaurant specializing in organic vegetarian meals. Yet another became active in the anti-draft movement that was emerging in the Spring of 1980. And, one of the core members surfaced as a leader in a late 1980 vigil against the Diablo Canyon nuclear plant in Southern California.

═══════════════

These two long vigils and the symbolic sit-ins described in earlier chapters raise an array of questions not previously addressed and to which we turn in our concluding chapter.

REFERENCES

Barkan, Steven E.
        1979   "Strategic, Tactical and Organizational Dilemmas of the Protest Movement Against Nuclear Power." *Social Problems* 27:19-37 (October).
Barnes, Paul
        1980   "Fractures in Anti-Nuclear Movement." *Sacramento Union*, March 16.
Cooney, Robert and Helen Michalowski
        1977   *The Power of the People: Active Nonviolence in the United States.* Culver City, CA: Peach Press.
Levy, Jacques
        1975   *Cesar Chavez: Autobiography of La Causa.* New York: W. W. Morton.
Rennert, Leo
        1979   "150-Mile Shadow of Seco." *Sacramento Bee,* October 13.
Sacramento Union
        1977   "The Reason: Security." January 26.
Sharp, Gene
        1973   *The Politics of Nonviolent Action.* Boston: Porter Sargent.
Widmer, George, et al.
        1979   *Strange Victories: The Anti-nuclear Movement in the U.S. and Europe.* Brooklyn, NY: Midnight Notes Collective.
Witt, Robin
        1979   "Protesters' Saga: Nuclear Foe's Persistence Born in Anti-War Days." *Sacramento Bee,* December 2.

CHAPTER VIII

CONCLUSIONS

We conclude with generalizations relating to seven aspects of symbolic sit-ins. The first three deal with their dynamics, discussing the "law of passive advantage" (section A), the surprising fragility of sit-in organization (section B), and the "preparation-event pulses" commonly observed in them (section C). The middle two sections give further attention to the historical origin and form of symbolic sit-ins, focusing on the special place of the Capitol "civility milieu" in facilitating them (section D) and on the inherent ambiguity of the idea of a "symbolic sit-in (as well as of all social categories) (section E). Last, there are the unavoidable questions of their "effectiveness" (section F) and their likely future (section G).

A. THE LAW OF PASSIVE ADVANTAGE

Three aspects of the situation of symbolic sit-inners prompt us to formulate a modification of Donald Light's (1969) "law of passive advantage" in classic protest occupations. We will describe these "situational aspects" and follow with an explanation of the law and its modification.

First, sit-inners were very much "at the mercy" of officials. Their enterprise was almost totally geared to achieving meetings with what were defined as "relevant" officials and achieving satisfactory decisions by, or pledges from, them. While it may not have seemed so in advance and superficially, once embarked, sit-inners saw quite quickly that the advantage lay with the officials in (1) electing to meet with them and (2) deciding whether to concede or simply to "stall" in the many ways that were available. In having elected to post themselves on the premises, the advantages of officials set up anxiety and tension: "When is the meeting?"; "With whom?"; "What exactly will be said?" and so forth.

Second, officials had, for practical purposes, infinite time but sit-inners did not. This fact was unspoken between officials and sit-inners but clearly known to both. Officials could afford to "normalize" the situation as "just another meeting" in a day full of meetings. Sit-inners were not so comfortably situated and wanted to "get it over with" or at least to "get on with it."

Third, in having been rendered routine or normal in the setting, sit-inners could in theory remain in place the rest of their lives. When officials pleasantly stalled and otherwise sidestepped demands, there came to be problems of deciding among escalating the tactics of demand, redefining the demands, defining the response of officials as satisfactory and leaving, conceding defeat and leaving, or merely leaving. Since none got what they initially demanded while they were still on the premises, all had to engage in redefinition of their situation and, importantly, devise ways to leave with dignity. In the longer occupations, a key, if not the key, problem was how to get out without seeming foolish and losing face.

Together, these three situational features provide a nice variation on what Donald Light calls the "law of passive advantage" in protest occupations. Surveying leading episodes of student seizures of campus buildings in the middle sixties, Light's "law" refers to the superior situation accruing to authorities in being passively open to protesters while allowing them to act (or even encouraging them to act) in highly assertive fashions, thus tending to portray themselves as unsympathetic aggressors. The upshot of such passivity combined with budding aggression is the "stand off" in which the restrained authorities seem increasingly "reasonable" and the occupiers increasingly "unreasonable" (Light, 1969:81). In this way, "the longer the stand-off lasts, the more ground the protester's lose" (Light, 1969:81). Credibility and the appearance of reasonableness are not as problematic in the symbolic sit-in, but, with modified referents, the law of passive advantage is nonetheless at work. In some ways it operates more poignantly because even though the occupiers were not disruptive or destructive, they were ordinarily quite far from their homes and all the physical and social supports this implies, in contrast to participants in classic protest occupations. Authorities needed only to wait; that is, to act normally.

B. THE FRAGILITY OF ORGANIZATION

On the surface and at a distance, one might posit that relatively formal, enduring, disciplined and hierarchical organization is requisite to strategizing protest occupations, especially those that involve "sleeping over" for an indefinite series of nights. Organization moving in that direction is, indeed, evident in the case of the United Farm Workers which is a large and stable labor union with a relatively elaborate and paid staff structure. That staff core could mobilize members and sympathizers, albeit the mobilizations were for relatively short "shifts" and only for sporadic and brief periods (Chapter VII, section A.2 and A.3). Operating from their nearby lobbying office and performing the core protest occupation acts themselves, staff could (and did) keep the effort going.

Such stability of organization and commitment was, however, the exception. The three other major and longer-term occupations, described in Chapters VI and VII, were conspicuously more emergent, fragile and temporary-coalitional constructions. Moreover and also unlike the UFW, it was difficult to identify the leader, a feature decisively suggestive of their emergent and temporary nature. Instead, there was a circle of situationally shifting leaders. Among the deaf/blind (who, it may be noted, did not even have a name for their coalition), the person we have identified as "Bill" emerged as the de facto leader but he was by no means formally the leader in press releases and in meetings with officials. Even his de facto leadership seems possibly an artifact of the unique circumstance that the other main leaders in the coalition were deaf and had difficulty speaking effectively in rapid paced exchanges with officials and among members of the coalition. The Title XX coalition was markedly stratified, certainly, but the organizations and persons that came together in the coalition could not entirely depend on one another to appear each day and the leadership circle itself had no formal head. That circle only labeled itself a "steering committee" and there was no "chair," "facilitator," or other such office. The anti-nuclear movement is ideologically anti-hierarchical, of course (Barkan, 1979), and the PUARS episode was conducted along the ordinary lines of that movement. "PUARS" was itself a label for a shifting cast of protesters (with, however, a fairly stable core) who were not a pre-existing group. Instead, they were drawn from several anti-nuclear groups in Northern California and formed a new "affinity group" for the occasion, united by their belief in the efficacy of occupying the Governor's reception room for the purpose of pressuring him to use his emergency powers to close a nearby nuclear plant. Following anti-nuclear protocol there was, explicitly, no single or small set of formal leaders (although temporary "spokes" were allowed) and all decisions had to be "put to consenses." Of course, as reported, the more assertive, energetic and articulate did emerge as a de facto leadership, but this was still quite different from ordinary formal hierarchy. As critics claim, there was, perhaps, a "democratic fog" (Widmer, 1979:14).

One consequence or at least correlate of these trends in social organization was interactional fragility. As coalitions of organizations and individuals and therefore very much volunteers for protest, continuing participation was quite problematic. People were exceptionally free to "pick up their marbles and go home," in a manner of speaking, and we have reported instances where components of the protests did just that. Indeed, the dubiously legal, clearly déclassé, and physically inconvenient actions in which they were engaging provided significant impetus to drop out.   One ironic upshot was that leaders seemed exceptionally polite to one another—almost gingerly polite.   None could "order" any of the others to do anything—to continue, to undertake a given action—and "natural" or "personal" leadership (as opposed to formal or bureaucratic leadership) became the basis on which strategy was forged. (We oppose only these types to each other because nothing remotely suggestive of the "magic" of "charismatic" leadership was observed.   On these and other types of leadership in social movements see Wilson, 1973:Ch. VI).

Other terms and phrases useful in capturing the organizational character of the longer term symbolic sit-ins include: tentative, groping, emergently negotiated, somewhat internally disorganized, and decentralized in terms of the factions composing the protest effort.

It is indicative, finally, that after their respective protest efforts, only the United Farm Workers continued to be locateable as an organizational entity.   The deaf/blind and the Title XX coalitions disappeared, as entities, the night its participants left the Capitol. PUARS persisted a few more weeks but then disbanded.

C. PREPARATION-EVENT PULSES

Many of the protest occupations we have reviewed exhibit a "pulse" feature in which the protesters launch an action, receive the response of officials, pause, launch a new action in response to that response, and so on to one or another type of termination.   While displayed perhaps most dramatically by the spirited siege of the Title XX coalition it is seen less conspicuously in other episodes and in most prolonged fashion in the PUARS vigil recounted in the last chapter.   The features of these "pulsations" emerge clearly by asking: "Toward what are the occupiers most proximately aiming?"   In general, the answer is: "Toward a meeting with officials in which demands are made and negotiated."   Such meetings require, in turn, preparation. Decisions about what to demand, how to demand it, and how to support contentions need to be strategized in advance of actual meetings.   Focusing on the PUARS vigil as a prototypical instance, we find it to have been structured around a series of five key and structuring events (i.e. meetings) that initiated a pulse, that is, injected a surge of directed energy into the protest.   These are shown in the left-hand column of Figure 2 and consist of meetings with and promises by officials, it is of key importance to recognize.   Such meetings and what officials did in them structured the vigil along the particular lines it evolved.   Put differently, it might be said that the PUARS vigil ran thirty-seven rather than some other number of nights because of the particular spacing of and promises made at meetings by officials.   In this sequence, there is a certain "stringing along" quality that encouraged the hopes of the vigilers, albeit they were eventually demoralized and redirected their energies.

Figure 2

STRUCTURING EVENTS AND PULSE PERIODS IN THE PUARS VIGIL

Structuring Event	Pulse
	1. Preparing to and occupying the reception room.
1. November 29: Chief promises a meeting with the Governor.	
	2. Preparing to meet with the Governor.
2. December 4: Governor promises another meeting, on December 17.	
	3. Preparing to meet again with the Governor.
3. December 17: Governor refuses the main demand, gives lesser concessions.	
	4. Demoralization and reformulation of demands.
4. December 24: Meeting with Chief; new, lesser demands granted, final arrangement meeting set for January 2.	
	5. Preparing for final meeting, shift of focus away from the Capitol.
5. January 2: Final meeting; arrangement of details.	
	6. Overnight occupation of reception room ends.

The pulsing surges of new orientation and energy are shown in the right-hand column of Figure 2 where the interplay between structuring events and "pulse period" orientation can be seen. Briefly recapitulating, the initial pulse brings the group to the Capitol and the first structuring event, the meeting with the Chief on November 29th, at which (of signal importance) a meeting with the Governor is promised for December 4th. That promise provides a surge of focus and direction, leading up to December 4, at which time yet a third pause period is initiated, aiming toward December 17th.   The December 17th meeting precipitated demoralization and the scaling down of demands, building to efforts to extract milder concessions, an effort concluded on December 24th, at which time a final, detailed settlement meeting was set for January 2, thus providing an orderly interval for terminating the vigil.

Scrutinized from this distance, slowed down, and viewed in "pulse perspective," the PUARS vigil (as well as many other protest occupations) evince social motion that seems quite graceful, supple and supremely interactive.   Forging forth, protest occupations encounter resistance, take account of it, reformulate action and force forth once more. Successive expansions and contractions are rather sensitively calibrated to officials' responses and, notably, episodes draw to a close in ways and at times that seem reasonable to participants and sympathetic observers alike.

D. THE CIVILITY MILIEU AS FACILITATOR

We have documented ways in which restrained or "symbolic" sit-ins went forth in the California Capitol and mentioned several background features that help explain the emergence of these pattens. These include the facts that (1) sit-inners were promoting causes that themselves had relatively wide social support and (2) they tended to "play by the rules" established by the California State Police, restraining and channeling their protest actions (Chapter II, section A). We want now to introduce another facilitating feature, one peculiar to the California Capitol as a social milieu, one we may think of as an unusually strong milieu of civility.

In order best to appreciate this feature let us first highlight how many authorities treated sit-inners in much more than a merely tolerant fashion.   It is one thing, one might say, to permit or allow symbolic sit-ins (and a great deal of the response to them was of that sort), but it is quite another thing to provide them active and even affectionate support.   Major forms of this may be briefly recalled, the particulars having already appeared in preceding chapters. First, supportive officials often addressed rallys staged by occupiers as prelude to or part of their occupation, most notably in the cases of the United Farm Workers. Second, legislators, in particular, were prone to "stop by" the Governor's reception room and give brief "pep talks" to protesters, a phenomenon especially apparent in the blind/deaf effort (Chapter VI, section A). Third, in at least one instance, legislators even collected money and handed the cash directly to the occupiers (Chapter VI, section A). Fourth, well situated aides to high officials provided continuing advice and "rumors" of what relevant officials were doing or likely to do. Fifth, and more diffuse and all-pervasive, officials in general were impressively solicitous of protest occupiers in that they took occupiers quite seriously in the sense of agreeing to meet with them, to listen respectfully, and to discuss their demands. The Governor's Chief of Staff and the Secretary of Health and Welfare seemed to do a great deal of this kind of work and to be especially adept at it. They have been, indeed, ubiquitous players in several of the episodes reported. They and other officials were not infrequently subjected to relatively harsh verbal treatment but, overall, they "kept their cool," as it is commonly phrased, and "took it."

These and other aspects of officials' behavior make up a reasonably benign and permissive social environment in which to perform protest occupations. Occupiers may not have often got what they wanted, but they were at least treated with a considerable measure of dignity, low-level, minor, and erratic harassment by the California State Police notwithstanding.

Let us now put this in larger, milieu context. Solicitousness and civility in the face of distraught and frustrated citizens was a broad and pervasive feature of the Capitol milieu. Quite stressful contention is endemic to the political process and an ethos of super-politeness and patience had evolved as a means of dealing with, or covering over, the very real, sharp, and consequential matters at issue. People commonly had good reasons to be deeply distraught and the Capitol etiquette of coolness and restraint was geared to control it (Cf. Suttles, 1970). The civility accorded protest occupiers, therefore, was not a special treatment of them. It was simply the civility commonly accorded people with whom one disagreed. Ironically and appropriately, the dispute riddled Capitol environment had given rise to a norm of restraint in the face of abuse that permitted, protected, and perhaps even encouraged the mild degree of incivility on the part of protest occupiers one observed. Accustomed to conflict and disagreement and practiced in handling it calmly, Capitol officials were prepared to deal with occupiers as only somewhat more obstreperous people encountered that day.

In discussing the "civility milieu," it is also important to report that through all the episodes we have chronicled and a host of related and "lesser" ones we have not (including an unending parade of "crazies" who "had to see the Governor"), one person more than all others was the champion of civility at the California Capitol. This was the person we have referred to by her formal title, receptionist, and to whom we have dedicated this report. With the exception of vacations and brief times for breaks during the day, she was the person regularly at the Capitol who had the most contact with protesters, serving in her role for all the six years that have concerned us and for several years before and after those six years.

The calm, friendly and supportive seriousness with which she met and dealt with aggrieved and distraught person after person and crowd after crowd was, to us, astonishing. To use a worn but telling cliché, she actually did "suffer fools gladly" and more than gladly. Her calm, seemingly imperturbable demeanor might be seen as, also, important (if not critical) in containing scenes a less composed presence might have aggravated. Leaders of the most "spirited" of "seiges" (The Title XX Coalition, described in Chapter VI) even sent her a gift and card of thanks after their protest in order to express their appreciation for her friendly treatment of them! It is indicative, moreover, that only once in more than a decade did she use the foot-activated police-alarm beneath her desk (and in response to a "pack-in" the members of which began to surge through a momentarily open door leading to the Governor's private office).

It must of course be acknowledged that she was not a decision-maker in the substantive matters that activated protesters and it was therefore easier for her to be civil; she was not a target of protesters' strongest demands and interactional abuses. Neither, however, were a large portion of other employees with whom protesters had contact at the Capitol who were civil, to be sure, but who not infrequently and nonetheless communicated a civility mixed with under and overtones of impatience, boredom, condescension and even contempt. We never observed any such sentiment on the part of our Champion of Civility and in repeated personal conversations and interviews with her we were convinced that she was in fact and sincerely sympathetic to virtually everyone in the bewildering array of people who paraded into and through the reception room of the Governor's office.

E.   REALITY AND DEPICTIONS

Categorizations of social experience unavoidably simplify what is in fact a more ambiguous "slippery," shifting, raw reality than the one depicted by thought-constructs. Such is the case for what we caption the "symbolic sit-in" as opposed to those that are more "substantial." In messy reality, many of the substantial protest occupations in the classic waves (Chapter I, section C) do not fall clearly into one or the other of the categorical-opposites we have pictured. Instead, they share features of both.

This occurs both in terms of the place in "wave" that an occupation appears (the later ones being more symbolic) and in terms of the life of a single episode when authorities and protesters negotiate a reconstitution of a substantial into a symbolic sit-in. Although occurring rather early in its historical wave, such a negotiated reconstitution seems, for example, to have happened in the student occupation of the University of Chicago administration building in May of 1966 (Light, 1969). Hints of evolving symbolic aspects are seen also in anti-nuclear actions. Activist-journalist Harvey Wasserman thus describes an August 22, 1976 Seabrook occupation in these terms:

> We told the police everything we planned to do and gave them no reason to mistrust our word...Everyone had a reasonably good idea of what was about to happen. There was an air of good feeling and self-assurance among both the police and occupiers that made the event seem more like a ballet than a traditional political confrontation (Wasserman, 1979:150).

Likewise, some of the episodes we have described here on occasion moved toward the more "substantial" or classic form of the protest occupation. It is only for the purpose of clarifying major patterns and dominant tendencies that simplifications of the kind we have practiced in this report are justified.

One important implication of this ever-problematic relation between reality and depiction is that we must be continually alert for evolving new patterns whose recognition is inhibited by the forcefulness of existing typifications.

F. EFFECTIVENESS AND EFFECTS

The single most important question to practical, political actors about protest occupations is likely: "But is it effective?" Or: "how effective is it in its several forms relative to other types of political action, especially relative to 'polite politics'?"

Such specific questions of effectiveness raise the general question of "how do we assess the effects of action?" It happens that scientific assessment of the effects of action in on-going, natural settings is no mean task. Causal assessment requires, at the most rudimentary, that a situation be "played through" identically in at least two forms, once with and once without the action in question. The requirement of identicality in all but the questioned regard is virtually impossible to meet in any but the most controlled and artificial of circumstances, circumstances that can and are created for a myriad of laboratory purposes but which are virtually never achieved in human social life (Campbell and Stanley, 1966).

In actual human life, situations are never "the same," or at least we dare not assume they are the same, because some other variable (or variables) might actually account for the correlation we observe between a social action and an effect.

Despite the unassailable truth of the proposition we can never have confidence in statements about causal links between social actions and effects in natural settings, it is also clearly unacceptable. People almost literally demand assessment of the effectiveness and effects of tactical actions in the social struggle; for, it is of enormous practical import. Sensitive to that demand, we elect mildly to pander and we do so with a clear vision that what we say has no solid basis and can never have any, for the reasons already stated.   Let us, then, speculate.

We begin by distinguishing "effectiveness" and "effects." By effectiveness we refer to assessment of the relation between the declared goals of symbolic sit-ins and their achievements over the reasonably short-run—a space of weeks.   By "effects" we refer to all other consequences of symbolic sit-ins.

(1) At the level of effectiveness so defined, we would have to say that symbolic sit-ins were extremely "ineffective." No one, in the space of weeks, got what they started out to get.

But perhaps this is too strict a measure of effectiveness. For, in processes of negotiation, some efforts got "lesser settlements" in the short run, settlements that the protesters, at least, attributed to their protest efforts.   For example, the deaf/blind coalition got access to high-level decision-makers, influence in the operation of an advisory council, and so forth.   PUARS got the items we enumerated even if their main objective, the closing of a nuclear plant, was not achieved.

This may, however, also be too strict a measure of effectiveness. Many episodes apeared not even to achieve a "lesser settlement" in the short run, but need not be counted as total failures. Social life is more complicated than that.   Even if a short run failure, the fact of having made an appearance, of having mounted a presence contributes to framing, in authorities' minds, a context for policy making.   For example, the angry gasoline dealers who packed the Governor's reception room (Chapter III, section C) failed to achieve any immediate policy changes (or even to see the Governor), but they did provide one more, however small (but dramatic), piece making up the interest group struggle picture that authorities (and others) would likely take into account when making subsequent decisions.   At this broader level, effectiveness consists of being perceived as present, as a player in the arena, as one of the forces that builds the agenda of social concerns (Cobb and Elder, 1972). Achieving such a presence probably requires much more than an occasional symbolic sit-in but even such a sit-in can dramatize an otherwise inconspicuous, sporadic, and unnoticed Capitol residence.

(2)   As we expand the meaning of effectiveness, we begin to overlap with the encompassing question of "effects."

The first question about effects is: "Effects on what?"   Without pretense to comprehensiveness, several salient classes can be mentioned. (a) One of these has already been discussed in Chapter II (section D) under the rubric "social reaction."   There we chronicled that effects on the media and citizenry seemed to run largely to bemused interest.   We can now go a bit further and suggest that one function of symbolic sit-ins was to provide some expressive and humorous release in the midst of otherwise grim Capitol doings.   Symbolic sit-ins might have served tension release functions not dissimilar to those served by the surprising amount of "horseplay" and zaniness that took place among legislators, especially among members of the Assembly.   In a situation of quite intense but rigidly controlled conflict, comic and other expressive activity becomes a strong need and many outlets arise, symbolic sit-ins perhaps among them.

(b)   The social psychological and associated effects on the protesters themselves are difficult to gauge.   Degrees of embarrassment, fear, anxiety, and boredom were easy to observe but it seems doubtful that these were lasting emotional states for many, if any, protesters. No one was physically injured (or even underwent threat of it) so permanent traumas of that sort are unlikely.

A goodly proportion of especially leaders of the episodes are known to have been involved in poltical matters months or even years after their symbolic sit-in involvements.   None have appeared as conspicuous parts of more "extreme" protests, however, and several of those known to us have been involved in "polite politics" (Chapter I, section A) in subsequent periods.   That is, there is no evidence that symbolic sit-ins made leading participants either more radical or inordinately prompted them to drop out of the social struggle altogether.

(c)   As reported in Chapter II (section C), the editors of the Sacramento Bee (1977) editorialized their concern that symbolic sit-ins would somehow degrade the political process itself by "developing into a destructive tradition."   Neither of these appeared in fact to have happened.

We might conclude, then, that symbolic sit-ins were mildly effective in policy terms and had relatively modest effects more generally.   In so assessing, we imply a comparison, "mild" and "modest" relative to what?   There are several of "whats" and the judgment is the same for each: (a) doing nothing, (b) doing ordinary interest group lobbying and associated action, (c) doing violent struggle.   And for each, achieving "mild" or "modest" effects is not insignificant.

G. FUTURE OF THE FORM

In view of the fact that protests in the United States are only canvassed and compiled for relatively special purposes and for rather short periods (e.g. Etzioni, 1970; Bayer and Austin, 1971), trends in total volume are difficult or impossible to assess much less trends in various of the forms of protest we outlined in Chapter I. Recognizing this, we can only offer the impression or conjecture that the symbolic sit-in is increasing in frequency despite the fact that they seem to have decreased or even ceased in the setting where we observed them. Some reports suggestive of increase include the apparent widespread but "symbolic" occupations of post offices attendance to the draft registration days of 1980 (Beck, 1980) and the willingness of some nuclear energy agencies to permit long-term and non-disruptive occupations of nuclear-relevant sites, including one in Vernon, Vermont (United Press, 1980) and San Francisco, California (Perlman, 1980).

To suspect the possible increase of symbolic sit-ins is not at all to imply the decrease of ones that are more "substantial." The indications are quite the contrary. While not defined, attended to and reported in the dominant media of mass communication, protest occupations of the more classic sort continue to take place with some regularity as Americans and other nations move into the eighties. (This, at least, is the picture one forms from following the left-oriented press in America (e.g. In These Times, The Guardian, People's World, etc. See also Gitlin, 1980:Ch. 11; Terkel, 1980).

The legal aspects are of course critical to the frequency and even survival of the symbolic sit-in. The restraint of authorities in protest occupation situations that is reciprocated by the restraint of protesters, thereby creating the symbolic sit-in, also creates precedents of practice that might well be used in court cases to claim some type of legal status for, or right to, it. Indeed, legal briefs in support of the more substantial forms of protest occupations have existed for many years, notably the sit-down strikes of the industrial workers (Fine, 1969:Ch. 11) and the sit-ins of the civil righters (Waskow, 1966:Ch. 16). No special imagination or talent is required to rework and adapt these legal theories for the symbolic sit-in (and at least one law firm is known to us recently to have experimented along these lines). The artfulness of the arguments devised and the receptiveness of courts, then, are integral to future possibilities for, and the attractiveness of, symbolically sitting-in. It might conceivably achieve the status of leafleting, picketing, and striking, practices all reported to have been illegal at one or another time in Anglo-American history.

REFERENCES

Barkan, Steven E.
    1979   "Strategic, Tactical and Organizational Dilemmas of the Protest Movement Against Nuclear Power." *Social Problems*, 27:19-37.

Bayer, Alan and Alexander Astin
    1971   "Campus Unrest, 1970-71: Was it Really All That Quiet?" *Educational Record* 52:301-313 (Fall).

Beck, Melinda
    1980   "Signing Up--and Sitting In." *Newsweek*, August 4.

Campbell, Donald T. and Julius Stanley
    1966   *Experimental and Quasi-Experimental Designs for Research.* Chicago: Rand McNally.

Cobb, Roger W. and Charles D. Elder
    1972   *Participation in American Politics: The Dynamics of Agenda-Building.* Boston: Allyn and Bacon.

Etzioni, Amitai
    1970   *Demonstration Democracy.* New York: Gordon and Beach.

Fine, Sidney
    1969   *Sit-down: The General Motors Strike of 1936-37.* Ann Arbor: The University of Michigan Press.

Gitlin, Todd
    1980   *The Whole World Is Watching: Mass Media in the Making and Unmaking of the New Left.* Berkeley, CA: University of California.

Light, Donald W.
    1969   "Strategies of Protest: Developments in Conflict Theory." Pp. 74-100 in James McEvoy and Abraham Miller (eds.), *Black Power and Student Rebellion.* Belmont, CA: Wadsworth.

Perlman, David
    1980   "Diablo Canyon Plant Raring To Go." *San Francisco Chronicle*, July 28.

Sacramento Bee
    1977   "End the Sit-ins." July 1.

Suttles, Gerald D.
    1970   "Friendship as a Social Institution." Pp. 106-135 in George McCall et al, *Social Relationships.* Chicago: Aldine.

Terkel, Studs
    1980   "Across America There's a Flowing of Life Juices...A Long Buried American Tradition May be Springing Back to Life." *Parade*, October 12.

United Press
    1980   "Police Permit A-Plant Sit-In to Continue." *San Francisco Chronicle*, April 1.

Weskow, Arthur
    1966   *From Race Riot to Sit-In, 1919 and the 1960s: A Study*

of the Connections Between Conflict and Violence. Garden
City, N.Y.:   Anchor Books.

Wasserman, Harvey
    1979   "The Nonviolent Movement Versus Nuclear Power."   Pp.
            147-162 in Severyn T. Bruyn and Paula M. Rayman (eds.)
            Nonviolent Action and Social Change. New York: Irvington.

Widmer, George et al
    1979   Strange Victories: The Anti-Nuclear Movement in the U.S.
            and Europe.   Brooklyn, N.Y.:   Midnight Notes Collective.

Wilson, John
    1973   Introduction to Social Movements. New York: Basic Books.

INDEX

113